• DIE SPRACHZEITUNG •

ABITUR-WORTSCHATZ
ENGLISCH

Prüfungsrelevante Vokabeln mit Beispielsätzen | Niveau B1–C2

CARL ED. SCHÜNEMANN KG

TABLE OF CONTENTS

Vorwort 3

TODAY'S SOCIETY
Family structures 4
Growing up 6
Homelessness 10
Leisure 12
Relationships 14
Religion 17
Role models 26
Sport 28

ECONOMY, GLOBALIZATION & TOURISM
Business • Finance 34
Economy 38
Globalization • Trade 44
Migration 46
Tourism 50
Work 54

EDUCATION
Higher education 66
Learning 68
School 69

GOVERNMENT, LAW & POLITICS
Civil rights 78
Crime 80
Politics 91
Politics UK 102
Politics USA 104
War and peace 108

LITERATURE
Describing literature 112
Elements of literature 112
Literary forms 116
Theatre 119
Verse 120

MEDIA
Advertising 122
New media 124
Newspapers • Magazines 126
Publishing 128
Reporting 130
TV • Radio 134

OUR WORLD
Cities 138
Environment 140
Geography 151

SCIENCE, HEALTH & TECHNOLOGY
Biotechnology • Genetics .. 156
Health 161
Information technology 170
Robotics 174
Surveillance technology ... 176

THE USA & THE UK
USA 179
The British Empire 179
The Commonwealth 183

SOLUTIONS 185
British and American English spellings 191
INDEX 192

Vorwort zur 2. Auflage

Für die Vorbereitung auf das Abitur und andere Prüfungen im Fach Englisch brauchst du einen guten Wortschatz in der Fremdsprache. Er gibt dir Sicherheit und Selbstvertrauen in der stressigen Prüfungssituation.

Die Vokabeln in diesem **Abiturwortschatz** decken alle prüfungsrelevanten Themen ab, sodass du dir schnell den Kernwortschatz zu einem bestimmten Themengebiet aneignen kannst. Bei einigen Wörtern sind die Schreibweisen für britisches und amerikanisches Englisch (BE, AE) angegeben, soweit diese sich voneinander unterscheiden.

Wichtig dabei ist, dass du Vokabeln erstens regelmäßig lernst und zweitens in Zusammenhängen. Es nützt nicht viel, wenn du 1 × pro Woche versuchst, dir viele Vokabeln auf einmal zu merken. Es ist viel effektiver, wenn du dir täglich eine überschaubare Anzahl an Wörtern vornimmst und diese auch regelmäßig wiederholst. Du wirst sehen, dass du auf diese Weise in relativ kurzer Zeit deinen Wortschatz spürbar gefestigt hast.

Auch das Lernen in Zusammenhängen ist sehr wichtig: Präge dir jeweils immer den Beispielsatz gut ein, denn im Kontext merkt man sich Wörter meistens besser.

Außerdem wirst du feststellen, dass zusätzlich zur Übersetzung und zum Beispielsatz auch andere Wörter derselben Wortfamilie angegeben sind. Lernst du diese Wörter von Anfang an mit, erweiterst du deinen Wortschatz und kannst dich eloquenter ausdrücken. Solltest du außerdem einmal auf ein Wort stoßen, dessen Bedeutung du nicht kennst, kennst du aber vielleicht andere Wörter aus derselben Wortfamilie und kannst dir die Bedeutung selbst herleiten. In regelmäßigen Abständen findest du kleinere Übungen, mit denen du das Gelernte festigen und in neuen Kontexten anwenden kannst.

Viel Erfolg und gute Noten wünscht
die Englisch-Redaktion

TODAY'S SOCIETY • FAMILY STRUCTURES

to adopt adoptieren   **adoption** (n.); **adoptive** (adj.)
Apple boss Steve Jobs was adopted by Paul and Clara Jobs.

child care Kinderbetreuung   **to care for/take care of a child**
It can be difficult for poor families to find and organise child care.

to cohabit in eheähnlicher Gemeinschaft leben   **cohabitation** (n.)
Couples that are not married often just cohabit like married couples.

couple Paar   ≠ **single**
The couple had a daughter before divorcing in 1990.

to delay starting a family die Familiengründung aufschieben   **delay** (n.)
Women often delay starting a family to establish their careers first.

diverse verschiedenartig; vielfältig   **to diversify**; **diversity** (n.)
Today's family structures are diverse and include single-sex partnerships.

to divorce s.o. s. von jdm. scheiden lassen   **divorce** (n.) | ≠ **to marry**
What might have happened if Henry VIII had simply divorced Anne Boleyn?

extended family Großfamilie   ≠ **nuclear family**
Living with extended family is very different from living in a one-person household.

to file for divorce die Scheidung einreichen
A married couple that doesn't want to live together any longer may file for divorce.

foster child/parents Pflegekind/-eltern   **to foster a child**
Over the years, Miss Monroe's parents took in around 80 foster children.

gay homosexuell; schwul   **homosexual** (adj.) | ≠ **straight**
About one in 13 American women in their early 20s identify themselves as gay/lesbian or bisexual.

TODAY'S SOCIETY

to get custody of a child das Sorgerecht für ein Kind bekommen
Michael Jackson got custody of the children he had with nurse Debbie Rowe.

half-brother/half-sister Halbbruder/-schwester
Barack Obama has a half-brother in Nairobi.

household Haushalt
Married couples represent just 48 percent of American households.

lesbian lesbisch   **lesbian** (n.)
Ms. Williams, who has a lesbian partner, already has a biological child.

 1 *Find the correct endings to the sentences.*

1. A boy or girl who is looked after temporarily by people who are not their natural parents is a
2. If two people live together as a couple but are not married, they are
3. They want to separate officially, so they have
4. Uncles, aunts, cousins and grandparents are part of your
5. George has the same mother as me, but a different father; he's my
6. The legal right to keep and look after a child, especially after the parents divorce is known as
7. John and Nora have just got married but they don't want to start a family now, they want to
8. When Sarah went back to work after the birth of her son, it was difficult to find
9. After being single for many years, Tom and Carol were enjoying life as a
10. There are many different kinds of relationships today; families are much more

a) extended family.
b) couple.
c) half-brother.
d) diverse.
e) cohabiting.
f) filed for divorce.
g) foster child.
h) delay it.
i) custody.
j) child care.

1. ___ 2. ___ 3. ___ 4. ___ 5. ___ 6. ___ 7. ___ 8. ___ 9. ___ 10. ___

5

TODAY'S SOCIETY

marital problem Eheproblem **to marry; marriage** (n.)
After decades of marriage, they learned to work through various marital problems.

marriage Ehe **to marry; marital** (adj.)
If two people have been in love for years, marriage is a good option.

to marry heiraten **marriage** (n.); **marital** (adj.)
Couples that want to live together permanently often decide to marry.

only child Einzelkind
Britain is becoming a nation of only children, with almost half of all parents now having just one child.

same-sex marriage gleichgeschlechtliche Ehe
Ireland legalised same-sex marriage in 2015.

to separate s. trennen **separation** (n.)
Paul McCartney wrote Hey Jude for Julian Lennon after his parents separated.

sibling rivalry Rivalität unter Geschwistern
He built an eight-sided house to control the rivalries of warring siblings.

single parent alleinerziehende/r Mutter/Vater
Her mother was a single parent who worked when her daughters were young.

stepbrother/-sister/-father/-mother Stiefbruder/-schwester/-vater/-mutter
She had a preview of life as a mother while babysitting for two young stepbrothers.

widowed verwitwet **widow** (f.); **widower** (m.)
She lives with her widowed grandmother.

GROWING UP

adolescence Jugend(alter) **adolescent** (n.)
Adolescence is a time of great personal change.

TODAY'S SOCIETY

adult Erwachsener **adulthood** (n.); **adult** (adj.)
Having to live through puberty is all part of the long road to becoming an adult.

to answer s.o. back jdm. frech antworten
She was punished for answering her teacher back.

clique Clique **cliqueish** (adj.)
Everyone who has ever attended school knows about cliques – social groups that often cause conflicts.

to criticize/criticise (BE) kritisieren **criticism** (n.); **critic** (n.); **critical** (adj.)
He often criticized his teenage son for being out of control.

2 *Complete the sentences with words from these two pages.*

1. Mr and Mrs Jones were always arguing, and had to admit they had serious _____ problems.
2. As an _____ child, she had always wished she had brothers and sisters.
3. He was often lonely at school because he never managed to get into one of the _____ .
4. She married her girlfriend as soon as _____ marriage became legal.
5. Her father remarried, and she got on really well with her _____ .
6. Her husband left soon after the baby was born, and she faced life as a _____ parent.
7. The two brothers were always arguing about who was the best – there was a lot of _____ rivalry there!
8. Tom and Mary fought most of the time, so they _____ and Tom moved out.

difference of opinion Meinungsverschiedenheit
Differences of opinion between parents and teenagers take place almost daily.

driving licence (BE); **driver's license** (AE) Führerschein
Nearly half of British 17- to 20-year-olds had driving licences two decades ago, but only 35% do now.

to enter a new phase in eine neue Phase eintreten
My sons have entered a new phase of life in which they won't take my advice.

to fend for oneself allein zurechtkommen
Our children are not ready to fend for themselves yet.

to gain work experience Berufserfahrung sammeln   **to experience**
The internships let students gain work experience with major employers.

gap year Jahr zwischen Schule und Uni/Beruf
After school, young adults can take a gap year to work in the social sector.

to give s.o. advice jdm. Rat erteilen   **to advise; adviser** (n.); **advisable** (adj.)
If it was your son, you'd give him the best advice possible on his career.

to go through s.th. etw. durchmachen
It's hard to describe the kind of pain their families are going through.

to hang out (coll) abhängen
We're just a group of guys hanging out.

to lose one's temper die Beherrschung verlieren
His team lost to the small south London club, and he lost his temper.

to mature reifen; erwachsen werden   **maturity** (n.); **mature** (adj.)
Smith had a troubled adolescence, but seems to have matured.

military service Wehrdienst
Once he has finished military service later in the year, he will move abroad.

TODAY'S SOCIETY

to moan about s.th./s.o. über etw./jdn. schimpfen/maulen
I can't understand people when they moan about not being paid enough. There is more to life than money.

mood swing Stimmungsschwankung **moody** (adj.)
Internet addicts often suffer mood swings when they have to log off.

peer group Gruppe von Gleichaltrigen **peer** (n.)
According to NHS statistics, teenagers who do not fit in with their peer group often have a lower life expectancy than socially integrated youngsters.

3 *Write the English word or expression in the space provided.*

1. die Beherrschung verlieren _____
2. allein zurechtkommen _____
3. Stimmungsschwankung _____
4. Meinungsverschiedenheit _____
5. Gruppe von Gleichaltrigen _____
6. jdm. Rat erteilen _____
7. Führerschein _____
8. reifen; erwachsen werden _____
9. über etw./jdn. schimpfen/maulen _____
10. Jahr zwischen Schule und Uni/Beruf _____

pressure Druck   **to pressurise** (BE)/**to pressure** (AE); **to put under pressure**
Children are being put under too much pressure to succeed at school.

puberty Pubertät   **pubescent** (adj.)
When puberty comes, teenagers often become disorganised.

to rebel against rebellieren gegen   **rebel** (n.); **rebellion** (n.); **rebellious** (adj.)
He rebelled against his middle-class background and adopted a London accent.

to set up on one's own einen eigenen Haushalt gründen
When young men first set up on their own, their flats often end up a total mess.

to settle down ein geregeltes Leben beginnen; s. (häuslich) niederlassen
He settled down with a woman chosen by his parents.

to sulk schmollen   **sulk** (n.); **sulky** (adj.)
Two-fifths of parents said they have seen their children sulking after losing.

to take responsibility Verantwortung übernehmen   **responsible** (adj.)
Companies should take more responsibility for their advertising.

to tell s.o. off for doing s.th. mit jdm. wegen etw. schimpfen   **telling-off** (n.)
My father told me off for taking his car without asking.

transition Übergang   **to transition**; **transitional** (adj.)
This has been a time of great personal and professional transition for each of us.

voluntary work ehrenamtliche Arbeit   **to volunteer**; **volunteer** (n.)
She is doing some voluntary work helping the Boruca people to build a new village.

HOMELESSNESS

affordable erschwinglich   **to afford** (s.th.) | ≠ **unaffordable**
There is little affordable housing in London.

TODAY'S SOCIETY

charity Wohltätigkeitsorganisation **charitable** (adj.)
The Big Issue Foundation is a British charity that helps homeless people.

eviction Zwangsräumung **to evict**
They had prepared themselves for eviction with workshops on legal matters.

homeless obdachlos; wohnungslos **homelessness** (n.)
Many homeless people prefer open spaces, but most quite simply have no money.

hostel Wohnheim
Some homeless people spend winter nights in a hostel … if they can afford it.

4 *Complete the sentences with a word from the same family as the word in brackets.*

1. Energy companies should act in a way that is environmentally _____ . (responsibility)

2. Parents should try not to _____ their children at exam time. (pressure)

3. Untidy rooms and loud music are some of the signs of teenage _____ . (to rebel)

4. After the argument, she was _____ for several days. (to sulk)

5. He left his well-paid job and worked as a _____ at a youth centre. (voluntary)

6. There isn't enough _____ housing for people with low incomes. (to afford)

7. Private schools in the UK have _____ status. (charity)

8. They hadn't paid the rent for several months, so they were _____ . (eviction)

TODAY'S SOCIETY

housing shortage Wohnungsnot
Even shared flats can be expensive in London, due to the housing shortage.

landlord Vermieter   **landlady** (f.)
Many Hindu landlords in Mumbai refuse to rent to meat-eaters.

low-income mit geringem Einkommen
Many children from low-income families fall behind at school by the age of seven.

rented accommodation Mietwohnungen
Rented accommodation is out of the question for most homeless people.

shelter Obdachlosenheim; Unterkunft   **to shelter**
New York's mayor wants to pay poor people to leave the city, to save the costs of putting up homeless families in expensive shelters.

to sleep rough im Freien übernachten   **rough sleeper** (n.)
About 3,500 people in England sleep rough on any one night.

LEISURE

disposable income verfügbares Einkommen   **to dispose of**
Older people with a high disposable income can afford to go travelling.

do-it-yourself (DIY) Heimwerken
DIY is a popular leisure activity, especially among men. Some even manage to renovate their homes in their spare time.

leisure industry Freizeitindustrie
From giant cruise ships to huge theme parks and concert halls, the leisure industry has grown enormously in recent years.

leisure/spare/free time Freizeit   **leisurely** (adj., adv.)
Modern parents spend a lot of their leisure time doing activities with their children.

TODAY'S SOCIETY

mass entertainment Massenunterhaltung
Mass entertainment including television and computer games is big business.

to pursue an interest ein Interesse verfolgen   **pursuit** (n.)
The interests Josh pursues include sailing.

retirement Ruhestand   **to retire; retired** (adj.)
Going into retirement can be difficult for people who enjoyed an active lifestyle.

spectator Zuschauer   **spectacle** (n.); **spectacular** (adj.)
Large football stadiums can seat up to 100,000 spectators in comfort.

 5 *Solve the puzzle using words from these two pages.*

Across
1. To follow
3. A person who watches something, especially a sports event
4. If you can't buy a house or a flat, you live in _ _ _ _ _ _ accommodation.
5. Abbreviation for do-it-yourself
6. If you sleep outside, you sleep _ _ _ _ _.
7. A place where people who are homeless can spend the night
8. _ _ _ _ entertainment is entertainment for a great number of people.
9. The man you rent a flat from
10. If there is not enough of something, you say there is a _ _ _ _ _ _ _ _ of it.

Down
2. The act of leaving your job, often because you are old

13

TODAY'S SOCIETY

spectator sport Zuschauersport ≠ **participant sport**
Football is one of the world's most popular spectator sports.

to target s.o. auf jdn. abzielen **target** (n.)
Summer blockbuster films are targeted at teenagers and families.

travel industry Reisebranche **traveller** (n.)
Cruise ships with up to 5,000 passengers are revolutionising the travel industry.

RELATIONSHIPS

to ask s.o. out jdn. zu einem Date einladen
Michael was afraid to ask Jessica out because she came from a rich family.

to be close to s.o. jdm. nahestehen
Emily was very close to Nicola, but she didn't know what to say when Nicola's mother died.

to become/get engaged s. verloben **engagement** (n.)
Prince William and Kate Middleton became engaged during a holiday in Kenya.

to be in love verliebt sein
People who are in love spend a lot of time thinking about their 'love object'.

to be on the same wavelength as s.o. mit jdm. auf der gleichen Wellenlänge sein
Jack and Jill were usually on the same wavelength because they both loved walking.

to break it off Schluss machen
When Gilbert met Helen, he broke it off with Eliza, who took it very badly.

to enjoy s.o.'s company gerne mit jdm. zusammen sein
He was fascinated by her intelligence, but he didn't really enjoy her company.

to fancy s.o. (coll.) auf jdn. stehen
How can you tell if someone fancies you?

TODAY'S SOCIETY

to get on well with s.o. s. gut mit jdm. verstehen
He got on very well with his first wife. He said his heart died when she did.

to go on a date with s.o. s. mit jdm. verabreden
Going on a first date with a person you don't know very well can be stressful.

to go out with s.o. mit jdm. zusammen sein/gehen
They had been going out with each other for years before he asked her to marry him.

to have a crush on s.o. für jdn. schwärmen
Young people often have crushes on celebrities.

6 *Put the letters in brackets in the correct order to find the word that completes the sentence.*

1. Jack didn't enjoy talking to Tom; they just weren't on the same _____. **(heaewlvgnt)**

2. Daisy and Tim got _____ after dating for six months. **(ndaeegg)**

3. I don't play football, but I love watching it; for me it's just a _____ sport. **(rtestcpao)**

4. In my teens I had an incredible _____ on The Back Street Boys. **(ursch)**

5. Adverts on social media usually _____ younger Internet users. **(atgtre)**

6. I had been arguing a lot with my boyfriend, so I decided to _____ it off. **(akber)**

7. I love visiting other countries, so I would like to work in the _____ industry when I leave school. **(erlatv)**

to be heartbroken/brokenhearted untröstlich sein **to break s.o.'s heart**
Susan was heartbroken when her partner left her after 10 years.

hostile feindselig **hostility** (n.)
As his alcoholism worsened, he became more and more hostile towards his wife.

impersonal unpersönlich
The Queen meets thousands of people, so talking to her can be quite impersonal.

intimate intim **intimacy** (n.)
The book describes the intimate stories of happy couples.

love at first sight Liebe auf den ersten Blick
It wasn't love at first sight but it turned into true love.

to make the first move den ersten Schritt machen
In starting a relationship, men are usually expected to make the first move.

relationship Beziehung **to relate to; relative** (n.)
Cindy first entered into a relationship with Chris while they were both at school.

to row (with s.o.) (BE)/**to argue (with s.o.)** (s. mit jdm.) streiten **row** (n.)
The neighbours could hear the couple rowing noisily.

single allein(stehend)
Life as a single person can be hard because you have to do everything on your own.

strained angespannt **to strain; strain** (n.)
He has a strained relationship with his famous father.

superficial oberflächlich **superficially** (adv.)
The Tinder app makes use of the most superficial aspects of the dating scene.

RELIGION

Anglican anglikanisch
The Anglican faith does not accept the Pope as head of the church.

archbishop Erzbischof
Antje Jackelén is the Lutheran archbishop of Uppsala in Sweden.

atheist Atheist   **atheism** (n.)
Dawkins, author of The God Delusion, is probably Britain's best-known atheist.

to attend a religious service einen Gottesdienst besuchen
Three out of four Mormons attend a religious service at least weekly.

7 *Use words and expressions from these two pages to replace the underlined words in the sentences.*

1. John was <u>very sad</u> when his dog died. _____

2. After her affair, her relationship with her husband became <u>very difficult</u>. _____

3. The fans were <u>very unfriendly</u> to the visiting team. _____

4. They <u>fought</u> about everything: money, the children, and even where to go on holiday. _____

5. I think it's very unfair that a man is expected to <u>act first</u>. I think it's fine if a woman asks a man out. _____

6. The study says that <u>people who don't believe in God</u> are often less happy than believers. _____

7. Emily is very friendly and nice, but the conversations I have with her are <u>not very deep</u>. _____

to baptize/baptise (BE) taufen **baptism** (n.)
Most Christians are baptised as children, but some are not baptised until they reach adulthood.

belief in s.th. Glaube an etw. **to believe in s.th.; believer** (n.); **believable** (adj.)
Most religions are based on the belief in some form of life after death.

Bible Bibel **biblical** (adj.)
Luther translated the Bible into German.

bishop Bischof
St Peter was the first bishop of Rome, meaning he was also the first pope.

Buddhism Buddhismus **Buddha; Buddhist** (n.; adj.)
Buddhism is becoming more popular thanks to the charismatic Dalai Lama.

Catholic katholisch **Catholicism** (n.)
The Roman Catholic Church is based in the Vatican in Rome.

Christian Christ **Christianity** (n.)
There are about 2.2 billion Christians throughout the world, making their belief system by far the largest global religion.

Christian values christliche Werte
Key Christian values include love, respect and faith.

church attendance Kirchgang; Gottesdienstbesuch **to attend**
Church attendance in Ireland has dropped dramatically.

Church of England anglikanische Kirche
The Church of England was created by Henry VIII.

churchgoer Kirchgänger **to go to church; churchgoing** (adj.)
John F Kennedy was a Roman Catholic and a regular churchgoer.

commitment to s.th. Bekenntnis zu etw.   **to commit to s.th.; committed** (adj.)
Martin Luther's commitment to Rome was destroyed by scandals in the Holy City.

communion Kommunion
Catholic children take their holy communion at around seven years of age.

community Gemeinschaft   **communal** (adj.)
Holmes County, Ohio, is home to the largest Amish community in the US.

confession Beichte   **to confess; confessional** (adj.)
Going to confession is part of the Catholic ritual.

 8 *Complete the grid with words from the word families. A dash (–) means you don't have to find a word.*

noun	verb	adjective
Bible	–	
Christian	–	
churchgoer		
	to attend	–
	to believe	
commitment		
community	–	
	to baptise	–
	to confess	

TODAY'S SOCIETY

confirmation Konfirmation   **to confirm**
Confirmation involves being accepted as a full member of your Christian community.

conscience Gewissen   **conscientious** (adj.)
Fighting in Vietnam went against Muhammad Ali's conscience.

to convert to konvertieren zu   **conversion** (n.); **convert** (n.)
Muhammad Ali converted to Islam as a young man.

devout fromm   **devotion** (n.)
Michael Jackson's mother was a devout Jehovah's Witness.

evangelical bibeltreu; evangelikal   **evangelism** (n.)
At present, evangelical Christians in the US are facing a 'Galileo moment' over the literal truth of the Bible.

extremism Extremismus   **extremist** (n./adj.)
Religious extremism sometimes leads to terrorism.

faith Glaube   **faithful** (adj.)
Having faith is one thing. Terrorising others with your beliefs is another.

fanatic Fanatiker   **fanaticism** (n.); **fanatical** (adj.)
In the time of the crusades, Christianity in Europe was dominated by fanatics.

freedom of thought Gedankenfreiheit
One of the first European monarchs to allow his subjects to practice freedom of thought was Frederick the Great of Prussia.

fundamentalist Fundamentalist   **fundamental** (adj.); **fundamentalist** (adj.)
Christian fundamentalist schools are teaching children that creationism is fact.

heaven Himmel   **heavenly** (adj.)
Pope Francis tells atheists: you don't have to believe in God to go to heaven.

TODAY'S SOCIETY

hell Hölle **hellish** (adj.)
Her son told her that she would burn in hell for drinking wine.

holy heilig
Rome is also known as the Holy City because it is home to the Pope.

humanity Menschheit; Menschlichkeit **humanism** (n.); **humanitarian** (adj.)
Christians believe the death of Jesus was part of God's plan to save humanity.

hymn Hymne **hymnal** (adj.)
The remembrance service for the victims of the Titanic disaster ended with the hymn 'Nearer My God to Thee'.

9 Use the parts of words below to make words that replace the question marks.

ven • out • firm • ity • con • hum • dev • ought • con • vert • science • ation • th • con • an • hea

1. Sandra was brought up as a Protestant but later she decided to ? to Catholicism.

2. After he stole the sweets he had a very guilty ? .

3. Mary was a very ? Christian who went to church every day.

4. The idea of ? as a place where you go after death is very comforting.

5. Freedom of ? would be undermined if her article wasn't printed.

6. The whole family went to the church for Daisy's ? .

7. The general was accused of crimes against ? .

Use the letters in the blue squares to find a word for someone who has extreme beliefs.

___ ___ ___ ___ ___ ___ ___ ___ ___ ___

immoral unmoralisch **immorality** (n.)
It's immoral to steal.

in private privat ≠ **in public**
Some people feel more comfortable praying in private.

Jew Jude/Jüdin **Judaism** (n.); **Jewish** (adj.)
She hadn't even known that she was a Jew until the Nazis took power in Berlin.

justice Gerechtigkeit **just** (adj.) ≠ **injustice**
Our country believes in freedom and justice.

Koran/Quaran/Qu'ran Koran
The Koran says that Adam and Eve were the first humans.

Lutheran evangelisch-lutherisch
Christians in the northern half of Germany mostly belong to the Lutheran Church.

mass Messe
Attending mass is no longer important to many young Christians.

miracle Wunder **miraculous** (adj.)
The healing of Lazarus was one of the many miracles performed by Jesus Christ.

mission Mission **missionary** (adj.)
Christian missions have helped many Africans, but they have also radically changed their traditional cultures.

monastery Kloster **monastic** (adj.)
Henry VIII had most of the monasteries in Britain destroyed.

monk Mönch
Martin Luther was a monk before he became a reformer.

Mormon Mormone
The Mormon church teaches members not to drink alcohol.

TODAY'S SOCIETY

mosque Moschee
A large mosque that is being built in Cologne has caused controversy.

national holiday Feiertag
Christmas is a national holiday in many countries.

nonbeliever Nichtgläubiger   ≠ **believer**
Mark Twain was not only a great satirist but also a great nonbeliever.

? 10 *Write the English word or expression in the space provided.*

1. unmoralisch   _____

2. Gerechtigkeit   _____

3. Feiertag   _____

4. Messe   _____

5. Kloster   _____

6. privat   _____

7. Moschee   _____

8. Wunder   _____

9. Nichtgläubiger   _____

10. Mönch   _____

23

nun Nonne
Perhaps the best-known nun of the 20th century was Mother Theresa of Calcutta.

observance (Religions-)Ausübung **to observe; observation** (n.)
They believe that children should not be made to take part in religious observance.

persecution Verfolgung **to persecute**
Muslims living in Hindu communities are often confronted with persecution.

pledge of allegiance Treueschwur **to pledge**
You have to take a pledge of allegiance to the state before starting this job.

Pope Papst **papal** (adj.)
Pope Francis is seen to be giving the Roman Catholic Church a new direction.

practice Ausübung **to practise** (BE); **to practice** (AE)
Going to church regularly is a central part of religious practice for many Catholics.

prayer Gebet **to pray**
I get on my knees every day to say a prayer.

to preach predigen **preacher** (n.); **preachy** (adj.)
Martin Luther King was a minister known for preaching some fine sermons.

priest Priester(in)
On March 12, 1994, the Church of England ordained 32 women as priests.

Protestant protestantisch
The Protestant Reformation started in 1517 after Luther nailed 95 theses on the church door in the town of Wittenberg.

religious affiliation Glaubenszugehörigkeit **to be affiliated**
Many American summer camps have a religious affiliation.

religious belief religiöser Glaube
You should be allowed to practise your religious beliefs if they do not hurt others.

religious denomination Religionszugehörigkeit
Roman Catholics make up the largest religious denomination in the US Congress.

sacred heilig
Hindus consider cows to be sacred animals.

sectarian konfessionell; religiös motiviert
Sectarian violence between Catholics and Protestants in Northern Ireland caused thousands of deaths.

 11 *Match each word or phrase with its translation.*

1. konfessionell
2. Priester(in)
3. Gebet
4. Glaubenszugehörigkeit
5. Treueschwur
6. heilig
7. (Religions-)Ausübung
8. Verfolgung
9. Ausübung
10. protestantisch
11. religiöser Glaube
12. predigen
13. Nonne
14. Religionszugehörigkeit
15. Papst

a) nun
b) observance
c) persecution
d) pledge of allegiance
e) Pope
f) practice
g) prayer
h) to preach
i) priest
j) religious affiliation
k) Protestant
l) religious belief
m) religious denomination
n) sacred
o) sectarian

1. ___ 2. ___ 3. ___ 4. ___ 5. ___ 6. ___ 7. ___ 8. ___ 9. ___

10. ___ 11. ___ 12. ___ 13. ___ 14. ___ 15. ___

secular weltlich ≠ **religious**
Turkey's religious-secular divide is as old as the republic itself.

separation of church and state Trennung von Kirche und Staat **to separate**
The separation of church and state is central to the concept of US democracy.

sermon Predigt **to sermonize/to sermonise** (BE)
I used to regularly fall asleep during Father Walshe's boring sermons.

set of values Wertesystem **to value s.th.; valuable** (adj.)
Religious education aims to give children a set of values to live by.

spiritual geistlich **spirituality** (n.)
Prayer is an important part of a religious person's spiritual life.

to violate s.th. etw. missachten **violation** (n.)
The schools admitted to violating the separation of church and state.

to worship s.o./s.th. jdn./etw. anbeten

worship (n.); **worshipper** (n.); **worshipful** (adj.)
On Easter Sunday, the Obamas worshipped at a church in Alexandria, Virginia.

ROLE MODELS

to behave inappropriately s. unangemessen verhalten ≠ **appropriately**
Some people drink too much alcohol and behave inappropriately.

compassion Mitgefühl **compassionate** (adj.)
Victims of crime should be treated with compassion and respect.

to emulate s.o. jdm. nacheifern **emulation** (n.)
Despite their beer bellies, men of a certain age try to emulate cycling stars.

to look up to s.o. zu jdm. aufschauen
Young people often look up to famous sports stars as role models.

looks Aussehen
Teenagers often worry about their looks, and so do many adults.

public figure Person des öffentlichen Lebens
US President Ronald Reagan first became a public figure in Hollywood in the 1930s.

trustworthiness Zuverlässigkeit; Vertrauenswürdigkeit   **trustworthy** (adj.)
Trustworthiness is key to working successfully with teenagers.

values Werte   **to value; valuable** (adj.)
Americans believe that older adults have better moral values.

12 Complete the sentences with words and expressions from these two pages.

1. He lost his job because he behaved _____ towards his female colleagues.

2. Christmas is one of the few days when many people go to church to _____ .

3. I don't think we should let David look after our funds; he isn't _____ enough.

4. As a _____ , the duchess had to get used to being followed everywhere by the press.

5. The priest gave a _____ based on the story of the Good Samaritan.

6. His father was a high-court judge and George wanted to _____ him, so he studied law.

7. She spent a lot of money on clothes and make-up because she was worried about her _____ .

8. As a teenager, he respected his football coach and _____ to him as a role model.

TODAY'S SOCIETY

SPORTS

adventure Abenteuer   **adventurer** (n.); **adventurous** (adj.)
BMX racing attracts young people looking for adventure.

to advertise (s.th.) (für etw.) Werbung machen **advertisement** (n.); **ad(vert)** (n.)
Sponsorship is a good way to advertise products from cars to sportswear.

amateur Amateur   **amateurish** (adj.)
Most athletes competing in the Iron Man are classed as amateurs, but some of them are just as good as professional athletes.

athletics Leichtathletik   **athlete** (n.); **athletic** (adj.)
The field of athletics includes events like the 100 metres race and the long jump.

ball games Ballspiele
Beachball and volleyball are the only ball games that work really well on sand.

to ban s.o. jdm. ein Teilnahmeverbot erteilen   **ban** (n.); **banned** (adj.)
Many famous athletes have been banned from sports for doping.

to beat/break a record einen Rekord brechen   **record-breaking** (adj.)
Every athlete dreams of beating a world record.

challenge Herausforderung   **to challenge; challenging** (adj.)
Athletes often accept challenges to test their limits.

championship Meisterschaft   **champion** (n.)
The World Cup Championship 2014 was won by Germany.

to clash with s.o. mit jdm. zusammenstoßen   **clash** (n.)
Hooligans often clash with the police.

combat sports Kampfsportarten   **to combat; combat** (n.)
Combat sports such as judo and karate are also known as martial arts.

28

TODAY'S SOCIETY

competition Wettbewerb **to compete; competitor** (n.); **competitive** (adj.)
The pupils will be invited to play in a football competition.

to disqualify s.o. jdn. disqualifizieren **disqualification** (n.)
Athletes caught doping can be disqualified.

to do sport (BE)/**sports** (AE) Sport treiben
Doing sports is very healthy, but it can take up a lot of time.

to earn one's living seinen Lebensunterhalt verdienen
Professional athletes earn their living from sport, but only a handful make millions.

13 *Complete each sentence with a word from the same family as the word in brackets.*

1. Usain Bolt is one of the greatest _____ the world has ever seen. (athletics)
2. The north face of the Eiger is one of the most _____ climbs. (to challenge)
3. The coach was inexperienced, and his training methods were _____ . (amateur)
4. Almost all the _____ managed to finish the marathon. (competition)
5. He gave up cycling after his _____ for doping. (to disqualify)
6. The new _____ for shampoo features football stars. (to advertise)
7. If they win the next two games, they will be this season's _____ . (championship)
8. Most of his _____ came from TV appearances. (to earn)

29

endurance Durchhaltevermögen; Ausdauer   **to endure**
Competing in a triathlon is one of the greatest tests of sports endurance.

equipment Ausrüstung   **to equip**
Most sports require special equipment such as a ball and hoop for basketball.

exercise Bewegung   **to exercise**
Getting lots of exercise is supposed to keep people fit, but some people overdo it.

exhaustion Erschöpfung   **to exhaust; exhausted** (adj.)
Finishing a marathon is a great achievement, but it leads to exhaustion.

fixed rules feste Regeln
Most sports have fixed rules. In football, breaking the rules can result in a red card.

to improve one's performance seine Leistung verbessern
Professional athletes improve their performance with special training programmes.

individual individuell/einzeln
Individual sports are suitable for people who value personal performance.

injury Verletzung   **to injure**
A study has found that 40 per cent of former NFL players suffer from brain injuries.

motor sports Motorsport
Motorbike racing is a classic motor sport that is very popular on the Isle of Man.

to obey rules Regeln beachten   **obedience** (n.); **obedient** (adj.)
We're going to tell people: 'These are the rules on doping – obey them'.

performance-enhancing drug leistungssteigerndes Mittel
Many athletes take performance-enhancing drugs, an illegal practice known as doping.

to protect oneself from s.th. s. vor etw. schützen
American football players protect themselves from injury by wearing helmets.

TODAY'S SOCIETY

to push s.o. to the limits jdn. an seine Grenzen bringen
The coach pushed the players to their limits during the training session.

race Rennen; Lauf **to race; racing** (n.)
The 100m race was won by Usain Bolt.

ref(eree) Schiedsrichter(in) **to referee**
A referee makes sure that footballers play by the rules.

14 *Put the letters in brackets in the correct order to find the word that completes the sentence.*

1. A 90-minute football match in the middle of a heatwave is a real test of _____. (**nareudcne**)

2. After his leg _____ he wasn't able to play for three weeks. (**jiyunr**)

3. The _____ saw the foul and gave the player a red card. (**eeeefrr**)

4. The test showed that the cyclist had used performance- _____ drugs. (**gnncnhaei**)

5. If you go on a diet, you should also make sure you get enough _____. (**cxrieees**)

6. After playing tennis non-stop for more than an hour in the intense heat, she was suffering from _____. (**theusixano**)

7. You don't need much _____ to play cricket; just a bat and a ball. (**nqpieuemt**)

TODAY'S SOCIETY

safety gear Sicherheitsausrüstung
Some sports should not be done without safety gear, such as a helmet for cycling.

sponsorship Sponsoring **to sponsor; sponsor** (n.)
Sports stars often receive sponsorship money for supporting brands such as Nike.

sporting event Sportereignis **eventful** (adj.)
The World Series is one of the biggest sporting events on the US calendar.

sportsman/sportswoman/athlete Sportler(in)
US gymnast Simone Biles was named 2017 Laureus World Sportswoman of the Year.

sportswear Sportkleidung
Special sportswear can make the difference between winning and losing.

stadium Stadion
Wembley is probably the most famous football stadium in the world.

to take s.th. up mit etw. beginnen ≠ **to give s.th. up**
A lot of young people are taking up extreme sports instead of traditional sports.

target sports Schießsport
Shooting and archery are known as target sports.

to televise s.th. etw. im Fernsehen übertragen
Big football matches are usually televised, but some are only shown on pay TV.

thrill Nervenkitzel **to thrill; thrillseeker** (n.); **thrilling** (adj.)
Mountaineering has always been popular with people looking for thrills.

tough measure harte Maßnahme
Tough measures have been introduced to prevent violence at sporting events.

tournament Turnier
Organisers say that 2010 was Fifa's greatest ever tournament.

urine sample Urinprobe
All professional athletes are tested for doping via urine samples.

violence Gewalt   **violent** (adj.)
Hooligans are known for their senseless acts of violence at football matches.

water sports Wassersport
Swimming is a cheap way of enjoying water sports.

World Cup Weltmeisterschaft
The 2014 World Cup took place in Brazil.

15 *Use words and expressions that match the definitions in brackets to complete the sentences.*

1. When Kane scored, all the England fans in the _____ cheered. (large sports ground)
2. Extreme sports can be dangerous, but people love the _____ they get. (feeling of excitement)
3. The tennis match was _____ so more people could watch it. (shown on television)
4. She was disqualified after her urine _____ tested positive for drugs. (small amount for testing)
5. The football club will not tolerate _____ by its fans. (aggressive behaviour)
6. Monica needed to lose weight, so she _____ jogging. (begin with)
7. The World Cup is the most popular international _____. (competition)
8. We will take tough _____ to stop doping. (steps, actions)

2. ECONOMY, GLOBALIZATION & TOURISM
BUSINESS • FINANCE

account Konto
Customers can transfer money automatically to other bank accounts.

accountant Buchhalter(in); Steuerberater(in)
Most musicians have no interest in running their own businesses; that's why they have managers and accountants.

to be able to afford s.th.   s. etw. leisten können   **affordable** (adj.)
She can't afford monthly payments much higher than $500.

amount Menge; Betrag   **to amount to**
Everyone has lost a huge amount of money.

to borrow money (von jdm.) Geld leihen   **borrower** (n.) | ≠ **to lend**
The countries borrowed huge amounts of money that they are choosing not to repay.

to go out of business das Geschäft aufgeben
In the last decade, more than 2,000 butchers have gone out of business.

chief executive officer (CEO) Firmenchef(in)
Mark Zuckerberg is the CEO of Facebook.

collateral Sicherheit
They used their house as collateral for a bank loan.

commerce Handel   **commercial** (adj.)
Millions of black South Africans still live in townships far from centers of commerce.

consultant Berater(in)   **to consult; consultation** (n.)
She is a paid consultant to ten drug companies.

consumer goods Konsumgüter   **to consume; consumer** (n.)
The direct sales company Amway specializes in cosmetics and consumer goods.

ECONOMY, GLOBALIZATION & TOURISM

discount Rabatt
Some universities are partnering with bike shops to offer discounts.

exchange rate Wechselkurs **to exchange**
The exchange rate is a problem: the pound is really down against the dollar.

favourable (BE)/**favorable** (AE) **terms** günstige Bedingungen
The terms were favorable to the banks themselves.

to found gründen **founder** (n.); **foundation** (n.)
She founded her company in 2014.

 16 *Solve the puzzle using words from these two pages.*

Across

1. A reduction in the cost of something
3. The opposite of "lend"
4. A quantity
5. The activity of buying and selling
6. To have enough money to pay for something
7. A bank _____ is where you keep your money
8. The top manager of a company is the chief executive _____
9. The exchange ____ for the pound will be very bad after Brexit.
10. A person who gives advice, especially to a business

Down

2. Adjective from "commerce"

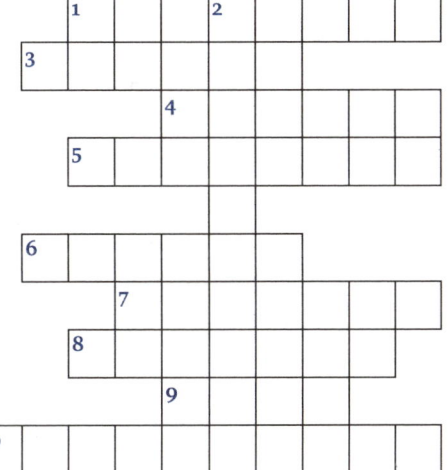

ECONOMY, GLOBALIZATION & TOURISM

human resources Personal ≈ **personnel (department)**
He was hired by the human resources manager, but the boss doesn't like him.

interest rate Zinssatz **to pay interest**
Low interest rates mean that the value of most people's retirement income has fallen.

to lend (s.o) money (jdm.) Geld leihen ≠ **to borrow**
Banks are not lining up to lend money.

to take out a loan ein Darlehen aufnehmen **to loan (s.th. to s.o.)**
Many students owe thousands of pounds in loans taken out to cover these costs.

market share Marktanteil
We have been focusing on the quality, not the size, of our market share.

merchandise Ware(n) **merchandiser** (n.)
The company gets merchandise from the design phase into stores within weeks rather than months.

monopoly Monopol **to monopolize/monopolise** (BE)
The Post Office lifted its monopoly on plain printed postcards in 1894.

profit Gewinn **to profit; profitable** (adj.)
With profits badly hit by the recession, the company plans to close about 960 shops.

to provide a grant eine Subvention bereitstellen **to grant (s.th.)**
The information will help in providing grants for those at the bottom of the caste ladder.

range Kollektion; Sortiment **to range from ... to ...**
His range of children's suitcases has become a huge hit.

retail Einzelhandel(s-) **to retail; retailer** (n.)
The retail market for games is hugely competitive.

ECONOMY, GLOBALIZATION & TOURISM

service industry Dienstleistungsbranche
Migrants to the UK often work in low-paid jobs in the service industry.

to soar rasch steigen ≠ **to plummet**
The cost of a full English breakfast is soaring.

to subsidize/subsidise (BE) subventionieren **subsidy** (n.)
The system provides subsidised food for the poor.

to undercut a price einen Preis unterbieten
The company dramatically undercuts the prices of traditional businesses.

? 17 *Write the English word or expression in the space provided.*

1. Marktanteil _____
2. subventionieren _____
3. ein Darlehen aufnehmen _____
4. Gewinn _____
5. Kollektion, Sortiment _____
6. Zinssatz _____
7. Einzelhandel _____
8. Geld leihen _____
9. Personal _____
10. unterbieten _____

ECONOMY, GLOBALIZATION & TOURISM

ECONOMY

austerity measures Sparmaßnahmen **austere** (adj.)
Many argue that the austerity measures have put the economy back by years.

bailout package Rettungspaket **to bail s.o. out**
Ireland received an €85 billion bailout package in 2010.

to go bankrupt in Konkurs gehen **bankruptcy** (n.)
Pepsi went bankrupt twice in the 1930s.

boom Aufschwung **to boom**
The construction boom is tied to this year's football World Cup.

to boost growth Wachstum ankurbeln
They hoped to lead the eurozone out of the recession by boosting growth.

budget Haushalt **to budget**
Public universities have been hit hard by deep cuts to state budgets.

capital Kapital **to capitalize/capitalise** (BE)
How much capital do you need to start a business?

to consume verbrauchen **consumer** (n.); **consumption** (n.)
India consumes over 800 million kg of tea each year.

consumer spending Verbraucherausgaben
Consumer spending on software is at record levels.

credit crunch Kreditkrise
Films take a long time to make, especially when there's a credit crunch.

crisis Krise pl. **crises**
My factory was hit by the economic crisis – it's been closed for two months already.

38

to cut taxes Steuern senken ≠ **to raise taxes**
Cutting taxes kept unemployment below one million for 30 years.

to be in debt Schulden haben **debtor** (n.); **indebted** (adj.)
Puerto Rico is $70 billion in debt.

decrease Rückgang **to decrease** | ≠ **increase**
The social network admitted it was seeing a decrease among teenage users.

demand Nachfrage ≠ **supply**
Universities have seen a 10% increase in demand for places this October.

 18 *Match each word or expression with its translation.*

1. Aufschwung
2. Haushalt
3. in Konkurs gehen
4. Kapital
5. Kreditkrise
6. Krise
7. Nachfrage
8. Rettungspaket
9. Rückgang
10. Schulden haben
11. Sparmaßnahmen
12. Steuern senken
13. verbrauchen
14. Verbraucherausgaben
15. Wachstum ankurbeln

a) austerity measures
b) bailout package
c) boom
d) to go bankrupt
e) to boost growth
f) budget
g) capital
h) to consume
i) consumer spending
j) credit crunch
k) crisis
l) to be in debt
m) to cut taxes
n) decrease
o) demand

1. ___ 2. ___ 3. ___ 4. ___ 5. ___ 6. ___ 7. ___ 8. ___ 9. ___
10. ___ 11. ___ 12. ___ 13. ___ 14. ___ 15. ___

ECONOMY, GLOBALIZATION & TOURISM

to collect/claim unemployment benefit (BE)/**benefits** (AE)
Arbeitslosengeld beziehen
A single person can collect up to £50.95 a week in unemployment benefit.

economic and monetary union Wirtschafts- und Währungsunion
Merkel said that her priority was to make sure that monetary union was matched by an economic union among eurozone members.

economic downturn Konjunkturabschwung   ≠ **upturn; upswing**
After the recession of 2008, the EU cannot afford another economic downturn.

economic growth Wirtschaftswachstum   **to grow**
These companies have long been seen as engines of America's economic growth.

economy Wirtschaft; Konjunktur   **economist** (n.); **economic** (adj.)
In late 2008, the economy was slowing down and moving into recession.

efficient wirtschaftlich; effizient   **efficiency** (n.) | ≠ **inefficient**
Growing crops for electricity was a less efficient use of resources than using that land for wind turbines.

essentials das Allernotwendigste
The government provides a safety net for essentials like food and housing.

the European single market der europäische Binnenmarkt
Free movement of labour is an important part of the European single market.

European sovereign debt crisis europäische Staatsschuldenkrise
Merkel has been rewarded for her handling of the European sovereign debt crisis.

financial crisis Finanzkrise
Many have lost their jobs as a result of the financial crisis.

goods Waren
Sales taxes on some goods have been cut in recent weeks.

ECONOMY, GLOBALIZATION & TOURISM

Great Depression Weltwirtschaftskrise
During the Great Depression, hundreds of thousands of Americans headed west.

gross domestic product (GDP) Bruttoinlandsprodukt
The company has contributed about 5 per cent to Ireland's gross domestic product in recent years.

income Einkommen
Transport for London will lose £70 million per year in income.

increase Anstieg **to increase | ≠ decrease**
They reported a 20 per cent increase in the number of Brits looking for jobs.

19 *Complete the sentences with words and expressions from these two pages.*

1. During the Great _____ millions of people were unemployed.
2. Economists expect an economic _____ later this year, but they say it won't turn into a recession.
3. China has seen very strong economic _____, which has lifted millions out of poverty.
4. People who lose their jobs can claim _____ for up to two years.
5. The car industry provides a large percentage of the country's _____ _____.
6. He only earned the minimum wage so there was no money for luxuries and sometimes, not even for _____.
7. George's _____ has risen by £1,000 this year.
8. In Europe, the _____ led to the introduction of the euro.

ECONOMY, GLOBALIZATION & TOURISM

inflation Inflation **to inflate | ≠ deflation**
The ECB has started raising interest rates across the euro region to fight inflation.

infrastructure Infrastruktur
The US is behind Europe and Asia in developing high-speed rail infrastructure.

investment Investition **to invest; investor (n.)**
Most of the businesses said they intended to increase their investment in China in the years ahead.

living standard Lebensstandard
Moving to cities allows migrants to raise their living standards.

manufacturing Fertigungsindustrie **to manufacture (s.th.); manufacturer (n.)**
Donald Trump promised to get American manufacturing back on its feet.

merger Zusammenschluss; Fusion **to merge**
The two companies are currently discussing a merger.

poverty Armut **≠ wealth; affluence**
Hackney, in east London, has some of the worst poverty in Britain.

prosperity Wohlstand **to prosper; prosperous (adj.)**
Good quality science and maths teaching will be the key to our future economic prosperity.

to raise s.th. etw. erhöhen **≠ to lower s.th.**
Since 2004, the government has been raising fares by one point above inflation each January.

to raise taxes Steuern erhöhen **taxation (n.) | ≠ to lower/cut taxes**
President Reagan was pressured by Democrats to raise taxes.

raw material Rohstoff
Problems with the supply of raw materials have left workers waiting to hear whether they will lose their jobs.

ECONOMY, GLOBALIZATION & TOURISM

property (BE)/**real estate** (AE) Immobilie(n)
Property markets around the country are cooling off.

recession Rezession
Sales are at their lowest level since the recession of the early 1980s.

to reduce poverty Armut verringern   **reduction** (n.)
We don't know how to use aid to reduce poverty.

share/stock Aktie   **shareholder** (n.)/**stockholder** (n.)
Burger King's shares fell by 19% last year, while McDonald's stock rose by 12%.

20 *Use the parts of words below to make words that replace the question marks.*

manu • ger • pov • fla • pros • erty • fact • mer • uring • perity • erty • prop • in • tion

1. Leeds in the north of England is a centre of the ? industry.

2. People in the slums of Mumbai live in terrible ? .

3. Unemployment was low and wages were high: it was a time of great ? .

4. Investors welcomed the ? of the two technology companies.

5. He made a lot of his money on the ? market, buying and selling houses.

6. Prices have been rising for the past few months: it looks like ? is back.

Put the letters in the blue squares in the correct order to find the American English expression for the answer to question 5. (two words)

___ ___ ___ ___   ___ ___ ___ ___ ___ ___

43

ECONOMY, GLOBALIZATION & TOURISM

single currency gemeinsame Währung
The EU is battling to control an economic crisis in its single-currency zone.

skills Kenntnisse   **skillful** (adj.)
We have seen an increased demand for workers with computer skills.

skilled labour/worker(s) Fachkraft /-kräfte   ≠ **unskilled**
Some employers are having a hard time finding skilled workers.

to spend (money on s.th.) (Geld für etw.) ausgeben
America's health care system spends nearly twice as much per person as Canada's.

to starve (to death) (ver)hungern   **starvation** (n.)
The government's inaction allowed up to four million people to starve to death.

stimulus package Konjunkturpaket   **to stimulate**
The president announced an economic stimulus package.

stock market Börse; Aktienmarkt   **stock** (n.); **stockholder** (n.)
Most American families do not invest directly in the stock market.

tariff (Einfuhr-)Zoll   ≈ **tax**
Reducing tariffs is now a priority for the whisky industry.

transport Transport; Verkehr   **to transport; transportation** (n.)
Delhi has 48 different 'modes of transport' including cows, elephants and camels.

unemployment Arbeitslosigkeit   ≠ **employment**
Fifty million jobs will be lost around the world this year, taking unemployment to 7.1 per cent.

GLOBALIZATION • TRADE

customs Zoll
The smuggler was caught by customs officers.

ECONOMY, GLOBALIZATION & TOURISM

developing country Entwicklungsland   **to develop; development** (n.)
Workers in Bangladesh and other developing countries are demanding higher pay.

free trade Freihandel
Free trade agreements have contributed to more regional movement.

global trade globaler Handel
Recent deals have played only a small role in the expansion of global trade.

globalization/globalisation (BE) Globalisierung
Trade deals are at the centre of the political debate about globalisation.

? 21 *Use words and expressions that match the definitions in brackets to complete the sentences.*

1. He made a lot of money by investing in the _____ . (where you buy and sell shares)

2. It hasn't rained for months and the fields are bare; already people are _____ . (to die because there isn't enough to eat)

3. The high-tech industry needs _____ in order to grow. (qualified workers)

4. The president said he would introduce _____ to reduce imports. (taxes on imports)

5. Many people in _____ don't have access to education and healthcare. (poor countries that are not industrialised)

6. The economy is booming, and _____ is down to just 4 per cent. (the state of having no job)

7. He hid the drugs in a secret pocket in his suitcase to get them through _____ . (the place at the border where travellers are checked)

ECONOMY, GLOBALIZATION & TOURISM

human trafficking Menschenhandel
His works describe corruption, human trafficking and organ trading.

industrialized/industrialised (BE) **nation** Industrienation
Studies show that Australia is the world's happiest industrialized nation.

to relocate umziehen; umsiedeln   **relocation** (n.)
English people who relocate to Wales may get tax breaks.

spread Verbreitung   **to spread**
The spread of English has reached almost every corner of the world.

trade Handel   **to trade**
Sales of film-related toys represent a quarter of the US toy trade.

trade agreement Handelsabkommen
The talks were aimed at creating the world's largest free-trade agreement.

trade barrier Handelshemmnis
If trade barriers were removed, production would rise in West Africa.

World Trade Organization (WTO) Welthandelsorganisation
Among developing countries, Bangladesh is the third-biggest exporter of clothing, according to the World Trade Organization.

MIGRATION

to assimilate s. anpassen   **assimilation** (n.)
For immigrants, trying to assimilate into British society was difficult at times.

(political) asylum (politisches) Asyl
Mr Putin gave asylum to American Edward J. Snowden.

asylum seeker Asylsuchender
Hundreds of thousands of asylum seekers arrived in Germany in 2015.

ECONOMY, GLOBALIZATION & TOURISM

border control Grenzüberwachung/-kontrolle
The EU has spent millions on border control between Turkey and Greece.

citizenship Staatsbürgerschaft   **citizen** (n.)
Some senators want to block the children of illegal immigrants from citizenship.

citizenship test Einbürgerungstest
One migrant group says the citizenship test is too hard.

country of origin Herkunftsland
The most common country of origin for yellow cabdrivers is now Bangladesh.

 22 *Solve the puzzle using words from these two pages.*

Across
1. To reach a bigger number of people
3. The state of officially belonging to a country
4. The country where you were born is your country of _ _ _ _ _ _.
5. Protection for someone who has left their country as a refugee
6. An obstacle that stops trade or makes it more difficult
7. To move to another place
8. Abbreviation for an international trade organisation
9. Word for someone who tries to get 5 across

Down
2. To integrate into another culture

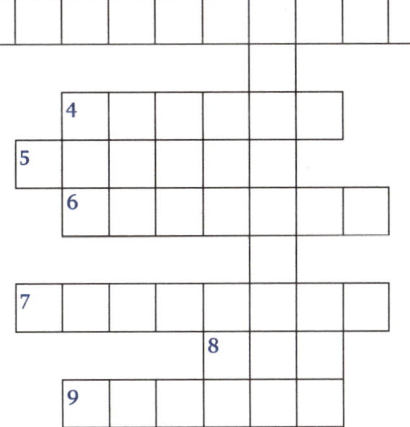

47

ECONOMY, GLOBALIZATION & TOURISM

custom Brauch; Sitte **customary** (adj.)
New immigrants typically bring some of their customs and culture to the US.

to deport s.o. jdn. abschieben **deportation** (n.); **deportee** (n.)
He is fighting to avoid being deported from his home in North Carolina.

descendant Nachkomme **to descend (from); descent** (n.)
Michelle Obama is a descendant of slaves.

detention Haft **to detain; detainee** (n.)
A record number of immigrants are being held in detention.

economic migrant Wirtschaftsflüchtling
The government says that most of the boat people are economic migrants.

to emigrate auswandern **emigration** (n.)
Ms Cruz emigrated from Puerto Rico when she was 17 years old.

to expel s.o. jdn. vertreiben **expulsion** (n.)
About 14 million Germans were expelled from the east after World War II.

famine Hungersnot **famished** (adj.)
Around 1.5 million people fled Ireland during the Great Famine.

to flee a country aus einem Land fliehen past tense: **fled**
She fled the country and hid in Canada.

foreigner Ausländer **foreign** (adj.)
There are about 460,000 foreigners living illegally in Arizona.

homeland Heimat
Britain is more attractive to many young workers than their homelands.

illegal immigrant illegaler Einwanderer
Most of the illegal immigrants in the US are Latinos.

ECONOMY, GLOBALIZATION & TOURISM

immigration policy Einwanderungspolitik
The country's immigration policy needs to be reformed.

influx Zustrom
The influx of international students has been especially important to the American economy.

mass immigration Masseneinwanderung
The industrial revolution brought mass immigration.

? 23 *Write the English word or expression in the space provided.*

1. Haft _____

2. jdn. abschieben _____

3. aus einem Land fliehen _____

4. auswandern _____

5. Hungersnot _____

6. illegaler Einwanderer _____

7. Zustrom _____

8. Brauch; Sitte _____

9. Ausländer _____

10. Nachkomme _____

ECONOMY, GLOBALIZATION & TOURISM

(ethnic) minority (ethnische) Minderheit   ≠ **majority**
In 2011, people of Indian background made up the largest ethnic minority in the UK.

naturalization/naturalisation (BE) Einbürgerung
To become an American citizen, you have to pass a naturalization test.

passport Reisepass
The EU has created a passport-free travel area.

to become a permanent resident
eine unbefristete Aufenthaltsgenehmigung erhalten   ≠ **temporary resident**
She became a permanent resident in 2008.

refugee Flüchtling
Fremont is home to one of the US's largest groups of Afghan refugees.

permanent residency unbefristete Aufenthaltserlaubnis   **to reside; resident** (n.)
They applied for Canadian permanent residency in 2006.

restriction Beschränkung   **to restrict; restrictive** (adj.)
Restrictions on immigration are causing a staff shortage.

to settle s. niederlassen   **settler** (n.); **settlement** (n.)
Around 850,000 Cubans have settled in south Florida.

transit country Durchgangs-/Transitland   **transition** (n.)
Many refugees are waiting in camps in transit countries.

undocumented ohne Papiere; illegal
Mr Mendez is one of about 11 million undocumented immigrants in the US.

TOURISM

backpacking Rucksacktourismus   **backpacker** (n.)
Backpacking is ideally suited for people who enjoy travelling on the cheap.

ECONOMY, GLOBALIZATION & TOURISM

to book in advance im Voraus buchen
Booking in advance normally takes the stress out of your holiday.

to conserve s.th. etw. bewahren   **conservation** (n.); **conservationist** (n.)
The idea behind ecotourism is to conserve the natural world while still having fun.

cross-country skiing Skilanglauf   **to ski; skier** (n.)
Sweden is probably the best place in the world to go cross-country skiing.

cruise Kreuzfahrt   **to cruise**
Going on a luxury cruise holiday is a very relaxing experience.

24 *Complete the sentences with a word from the same family as the word in brackets.*

1. After Chris emigrated, London became his place of _____. (resident)
2. In 1921, a law _____ the number of immigrants to 357,000 per year. (restriction)
3. Many of the early _____ in Australia were convicts sent from Britain. (to settle)
4. After they leave school, many teenagers go _____ around Australia for a year. (backpacker)
5. One of the most important areas of work done by the National Trust is the _____ of historic buildings. (to conserve)
6. Emily is a brilliant _____ although she only learnt the sport two years ago. (to ski)
7. The country is making the _____ from agricultural economy to industrial economy. (transit)
8. Jamestown Colony was the first permanent English _____ in North America. (to settle)

ECONOMY, GLOBALIZATION & TOURISM

destination Reiseziel
When planning a holiday, you should choose your destination carefully.

ecotourism Ökotourismus
Ecotourism allows you to visit beautiful places without damaging the environment.

environmentally conscious umweltbewusst
Environmentally conscious tourists don't get too close to wild animals.

to explore s.th. etw. erkunden **explorer** (n.)
Mass tourism lets ordinary people explore new countries on a low budget.

fragile zerbrechlich; empfindlich **fragility** (n.)
Coral reefs are quite fragile ecosystems.

to grow at a fast rate schnell wachsen **growth** (n.) | ≠ **to shrink**
The cruise holiday sector has grown at a very fast rate in recent years.

guide Reiseführer(in) **guidebook** (n.)
The guide takes about 50 people a day through Asia's biggest slum.

to have a negative impact e-e negative Auswirkung haben
Mass tourism can have a negative impact on the environment, as the required infrastructure can destroy entire ecosystems.

hiking Wandern **to hike; hike** (n.)
The students enjoyed hiking in the New England countryside.

the local community die örtliche Bevölkerung
The interests of the local community have to be balanced with the status of the town as a world-famous destination.

mass tourism Massentourismus
Thomas Cook is the company that started mass tourism in the 1840s.

native Einheimischer
New Orleans natives don't go to the city's French Quarter very often.

package holiday/tour Pauschalreise
Package tours are great for older people because everything is organised for them.

passport control Passkontrolle
People can move across most of the EU without passport controls.

popularity Beliebtheit   **popular** (adj.)
Iceland is growing in popularity as a destination for school trips.

 25 *Match each word or expression with its translation.*

1. schnell wachsen
2. Beliebtheit
3. Wandern
4. e-e negative Auswirkung haben
5. Massentourismus
6. Einheimischer
7. Reiseziel
8. etw. erkunden
9. Pauschalreise
10. Ökotourismus
11. Passkontrolle
12. die örtliche Bevölkerung
13. Reiseführer(in)
14. umweltbewusst
15. zerbrechlich; empfindlich

a) destination
b) ecotourism
c) environmentally conscious
d) to explore s.th.
e) fragile
f) to grow at a fast rate
g) guide
h) hiking
i) to have a negative impact
j) the local community
k) mass tourism
l) package holiday/tour
m) popularity
n) passport control
o) native

1. ____ 2. ____ 3. ____ 4. ____ 5. ____ 6. ____ 7. ____ 8. ____ 9. ____
10. ____ 11. ____ 12. ____ 13. ____ 14. ____ 15. ____

ECONOMY, GLOBALIZATION & TOURISM

to profit profitieren **profit** (n.); **profitable** (adj.)
It is hard to say whether the people of Venice profit from tourism.

to relax s. entspannen **relaxation** (n.); **relaxing** (adj.)
Most people go on holiday to relax after months of hard work.

resort Urlaubsort
Blackpool used to be a popular holiday resort with lower middle class Britons.

sports facilities Sporteinrichtungen
Most good hotels have sports facilities such as tennis courts and gyms.

sports tourism Sporttourismus
The Olympic Games have led to a rise in sports tourism.

tour operator Reiseveranstalter
Thomas Cook of London was the world's first tour operator.

transportation Transport; Verkehr **to transport**
Mass tourism cannot work without excellent transportation networks.

travel agency Reisebüro **travel agent** (n.)
Booking a holiday at a travel agency can be cheaper than booking online because travel agents know how to get the best deal.

WORK

absenteeism häufiges Fernbleiben von der Arbeit **absence** (n.); **absent** (adj.)
Large organisations tend to have higher levels of absenteeism than smaller ones.

(job) ad/advert (BE)/**advertisement** Stellenanzeige
Recent advertisements for female bus drivers received no applicants.

affirmative action Quotenregelung zugunsten benachteiligter Gruppen
India's four southern states have given some affirmative action benefits to Muslims.

ECONOMY, GLOBALIZATION & TOURISM

agriculture Landwirtschaft   **agricultural** (adj.)
A hundred years ago, most working Europeans were still employed in agriculture.

to apply for a job s. bewerben   **applicant** (n.); **application** (n.)
She applied for more than 100 jobs but got just two interviews.

apprentice Auszubildende(r)   **apprenticesehip** (n.)
Rebecca is the world's first apprentice bee farmer.

assembly line Fließ-/Montageband   **to assemble**
Vehicles will start rolling off the assembly line in June.

? 26 *Complete the sentences with words from these two pages.*

1. The tour _____ tried to get the hotel to reduce its prices for the coming year.

2. Guests don't need to worry about getting to the hotel: _____ from the airport will be organised for them.

3. The travel _____ has gone out of business because so many people book their trips online.

4. This year we went to a quiet _____ on the south coast for our holiday.

5. The hotel has great food, but if you want _____ like a gym or tennis courts, you will be disappointed.

6. The hotel is very quiet and doesn't have any entertainments, but it's perfect if you just want to _____ .

7. The locals have _____ from tourism, as it has created many jobs.

8. One in ten of the staff were off sick yesterday. We have to do something about _____ in our company.

ECONOMY, GLOBALIZATION & TOURISM

basic requirement Grundvoraussetzung **to require**
One basic requirement of the job is that workers be physically fit and drug free.

blue-collar worker Arbeiter ≠ **white-collar worker**
In some sectors, blue-collar workers can actually earn more money than junior doctors.

career Karriere
Generations of children followed their fathers to sea and a career in fishing.

to collaborate zusammenarbeiten **collaboration** (n.); **collaborative** (adj.)
Skills such as collaborating with others are required in many jobs.

competitive wettbewerbsintensiv **to compete; competitor** (n.); **competition** (n.)
The labour market is much more competitive today.

contract Vertrag **to contract; contractor** (n.)
Every three months his contract ends and factory bosses send him home.

co-worker Kollege =**colleague**
Bankers can have a video chat with a co-worker on the other side of the planet.

craftsman/-woman (Kunst)Handwerker/-in **craft** (n.)
The leather gloves were made by a master craftsman.

curriculum vitae (CV) (BE)/**resumé** (AE) Lebenslauf
Local businesses don't even really want to take my CV.

delivery time Lieferzeit
In some parts of the USA, delivery time for Amazon Prime customers has been reduced to two hours or less.

discrimination Diskriminierung **to discriminate; discriminatory** (adj.)
Women students viewed banking as the occupation in which they were most likely to find discrimination.

ECONOMY, GLOBALIZATION & TOURISM

dismissal Entlassung **to dismiss**
Workers are looking for ways of getting around the new unfair dismissal rules.

to **downsize** (s.) verkleinern; den Personalbestand verringern
She lost a series of jobs at small firms that had downsized.

to **employ s.o.** jdn. beschäftigen
Tourism employs 20 million people throughout India.

employee
Arbeitnehmer(in); Beschäftigte(r)   **to employ; employer** (n.); **employment** (n.)
The company had 100 employees a few years ago but is now down to about 50.

? 27 Use words and expressions from these two pages to replace the underlined words in the sentences.

1. The company's managers are very generous to the people who work for them.

2. George said his sacking was unfair and he would not accept it.

3. We get the best results if we work together with other departments.

4. Ms Smith has complained about unfair treatment because of her age.

5. John got on really well with his colleagues but the manager said he was lazy.

6. We need to improve our technology to keep up with our rivals in China.

7. This year, workers in production got a bigger rise than office workers did.

8. Peter lost his well-paid job after the company got smaller by reducing staff.

57

ECONOMY, GLOBALIZATION & TOURISM

equal opportunity Chancengleichheit
The country's economic system gives everyone an equal opportunity to succeed.

forced labour (BE)/**labor** (AE) Zwangsarbeit(er)
There have been reports of forced labour being used to build new airports.

freelance freiberuflich **freelancer** (n.)
They earn money by doing freelance work.

grievance (Grund zur) Klage
The grievances of London's hotel staff are very serious.

growth Wachstum
Small service-oriented businesses have long been engines of economic growth.

to hand in one's notice kündigen **to give s.o. notice**
When the boss asked his secretary to clean the men's room, she handed in her notice.

industrialization/industrialisation (BE)
Industrialisierung **to industrialize/industrialise** (BE); **industry** (n.)
Rapid industrialization totally changed British society in the 1800s.

interview Vorstellungsgespräch **interviewer** (n.); **interviewee** (n.)
She still remembers an interview that led her to leave the building in tears.

job creation Schaffung von Arbeitsplätzen
Smaller companies are the engines of innovation and job creation.

job security Jobsicherheit ≠ **job insecurity**
Many musicians have little job security.

labour (BE)/**labor** (AE) Arbeit(skraft) **to labour; labourer** (n.); **laborious** (adj.)
Men have traditionally done the jobs involving physical labour.

to lay s.o. off jdn. (betriebsbedingt) entlassen **layoff** (n.) | ≠ **to hire s.o.**
He spent 17 years at the company before being laid off in the 1990s.

letter of application (BE)/**cover letter** (AE) Bewerbungsschreiben
It's important to write a good cover letter when you apply for a job.

livelihood Existenzgrundlage
Global warming risks the livelihoods of millions of people.

machinery Maschinen
Small farms can produce food with less machinery and more human interaction.

> **28** *Use words and expressions that match the definitions in brackets to complete the sentences.*

1. The pay was too low, the hours too long and working conditions bad – the workers had many _____. (things to complain about)

2. Everyone gets the same treatment at our firm: we are an _____ employer. (the right to be treated without discrimination)

3. It is very hard for young people to plan their lives without job _____. (safety)

4. In developing countries, many people rely on farming for their _____. (activity that gives you enough money to live on)

5. I want to get this job, so I'm going to write a really good letter of _____. (a request for a job, especially in writing)

6. She didn't like the job, so after six months, she handed in her _____. (declaration that you want to leave your job)

7. Harry had worked for the newspaper for many years, but he left to do _____ work and have more independence. (work done for yourself, not an employer)

ECONOMY, GLOBALIZATION & TOURISM

to make a living seinen Lebensunterhalt bestreiten
Most Amish have had to find new ways to make a living.

manual skill handwerkliche Fertigkeit
Today, manual skills such as woodworking are not as important as knowing how to use computer programs.

manufacturing process Herstellungsprozess   **to manufacture**
Coca-Cola has updated its manufacturing processes, but never changed its secret formula.

to mass-produce in großen Mengen herstellen   **mass production** (n.)
The company's chicken and pork products are mass-produced.

to take maternity/paternity/parental leave Elternzeit in Anspruch nehmen
Marissa Mayer of Yahoo took only a few weeks of maternity leave.

minimum wage Mindestlohn
The jobs start off on minimum wage, but people work their way up.

to negotiate with s.o. mit jdm. verhandeln   **negotiation** (n.); **negotiator** (n.)
The winning institutions will now have to negotiate with NASA over the cost.

to outsource (a job) (eine Aufgabe) nach außen vergeben   **outsourcing** (n.)
All but the most important jobs in an Internet company can be outsourced.

overtime Überstunden
Some workers can earn $150,000 a year, including overtime.

part-time/full-time Teilzeit(-)/Vollzeit(-)
A study found that 1.26 million of those in work are in part-time jobs because they could not find a full-time position.

pay rise (BE)/**pay raise** (AE) Lohnerhöhung
I haven't had a pay rise since 2002.

ECONOMY, GLOBALIZATION & TOURISM

pension plan (betriebliche) Altersvorsorge
A third of African Americans do not have a pension plan.

personnel Personal   **= staff**
The players said they were improperly treated by medical personnel.

profession Beruf   **professional** (adj.)
It is difficult for women to rise to the top of the medical profession.

to promote befördern   **promotion** (n.)
Black coaches are less likely to be promoted than white ones.

? 29 *Write the English word or expression in the space provided.*

1. seinen Lebensunterhalt bestreiten _____

2. befördern _____

3. Herstellungsprozess _____

4. Mindestlohn _____

5. Überstunden _____

6. Teilzeit _____

7. Lohnerhöhung _____

8. Elternzeit in Anspruch nehmen _____

9. mit jdm. verhandeln _____

10. (betriebliche) Altersvorsorge _____

ECONOMY, GLOBALIZATION & TOURISM

promotion Beförderung **to promote**
Self-selling is great for people looking for promotion.

to recruit s.o. jdn. einstellen/anwerben **recruitment** (n.); **recruiter** (n.)
Some Australian companies are actively recruiting workers from Britain.

to be made redundant betriebsbedingt entlassen werden **redundancy** (n.)
Thousands of workers will be made redundant from the UK's banks within the next three years.

to replace s.o./s.th. jdn./etw. ersetzen **replacement** (n.)
With baby boomers starting to retire, employers worry there will be few young workers to replace them.

to retire in den Ruhestand treten **retirement** (n.); **retired** (adj.)
From 1979 until she retired in 1998, Ms Ledbetter was one of the few women managers at the company.

to retrain umschulen
The company closed for a day to retrain its workers.

to sack (BE)/**to fire** entlassen **to get the sack**
She was told that she wasn't fit for the culture of the company and sacked.

salary Gehalt **salaried** (adj.)
Most of his teammates earn salaries under $50,000.

semi-skilled angelernt
Most new jobs will be semi-skilled or technical.

senior leitend
He is a senior economist at Deutsche Bank.

to set up a business ein Geschäft/Unternehmen gründen
Eight years after Apple was set up, the Mac home computer was born.

ECONOMY, GLOBALIZATION & TOURISM

shareholder/stockholder Aktionär **share/stock** (n.)
The companies are building up loyalty by turning customers into shareholders.

to take sick leave s. krankschreiben lassen
More than a million people take sick leave for over a month each year.

skills shortage Fachkräftemangel
A sector that has a skills shortage can employ migrant workers.

to go/be on strike streiken **striker** (n.)
Workers have gone on strike over pay.

? 30 Complete the sentences with a word from the same family as the word in brackets.

1. The manager said there would be no _____, but there wouldn't be a pay rise either. (redundant)

2. Our secretary is leaving, so we need to find a _____ for her. (to replace)

3. Annette was _____ because of the excellent work she did. (promotion)

4. Workers who are paid hourly rates usually earn less than _____ staff. (salary)

5. After 37 years with the firm, she was really looking forward to _____. (to retire)

6. We are using a _____ to find IT staff. (to recruit)

7. Mark invested most of his money in _____. (shareholder)

8. The _____ stood outside the factory and protested against the layoffs. (to strike)

ECONOMY, GLOBALIZATION & TOURISM

supervisor Vorgesetzte(r); Leiter(in)   **to supervise | ≠ subordinate**
He started out washing tanks and today earns $300,000 a year as a supervisor with an oil field support firm.

supplier Lieferant   **to supply; supply** (n.)
The company is a leading supplier of musical instruments.

trade union (BE)/**labor union** (AE) Gewerkschaft
Labor leaders want the government to make it easier for workers to form unions.

vocational training Berufsausbildung
Britain is far behind countries like Germany in its use of vocational training programmes to introduce young people to permanent work.

wage Lohn
African Americans earn much higher wages in the auto industry than in other parts of the economy.

white-collar worker Büroarbeiter(in)   **≠ blue-collar worker**
In these turbulent times, white-collar workers in the US are almost as likely to lose their jobs as blue-collar workers.

work experience Praktikum; Arbeitserfahrung
Part-time jobs give young people practical work experience.

workforce Belegschaft; Erwerbsbevölkerung
In the 1960s, large numbers of Turkish workers entered the German workforce.

working hours Arbeitszeit
Almost a third of the employees want to cut their working hours.

31 Use words from the 'work' section to complete the crossword. Put the letters in the blue squares in the correct order to find a big IT company.

Across
2 All the people who work in a firm
5. and 12 across An organisation of workers
8. see 9 across
9. and 8 across Someone who works in an office
10. To tell someone they have to leave their job
11. A young person learning a job
12. See 5 across
13. Adjective for a job you do with your hands

Down
1. To stop working because you are old
3. Extra hours of work
4. A person who tells other people at work what to do
6. The money a worker earns
7. The kind of training that teaches you how to do your job

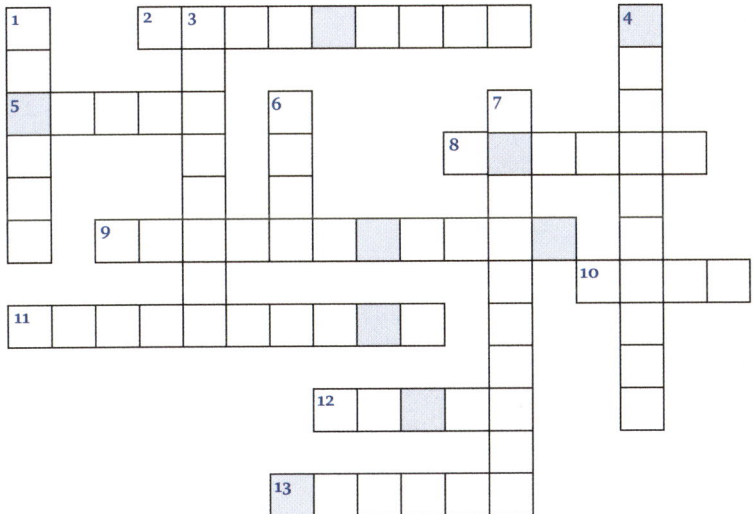

IT company: ___ ___ ___ ___ ___ ___ ___ ___ ___

EDUCATION • HIGHER EDUCATION

apprenticeship Berufsausbildung (im Betrieb) **apprentice** (n.)
Record numbers of pupils are doing apprenticeships instead of going to university.

to go to college (bes. AE)/**university** (BE) studieren
I plan to go to college in Wisconsin.

degree course Studiengang
Nursing degree courses are popular these days.

diploma Schul-/Universitätsabschluss
In the United States, girls earn more diplomas than boys.

distance learning Fernkurse/-studium
Modern distance learning programmes use the Internet.

financial aid finanzielle Unterstützung
Even with financial aid, he couldn't pay for college.

higher education Hochschulbildung
Oxford University is an institution of higher education.

humanities Geisteswissenschaften
People with degrees in humanities like history and literature have useful skills.

to major in s.th. (AE) etw. im Hauptfach studieren **major** (n.)
Supreme Court Justice Clarence Thomas majored in English in college.

qualification Qualifikation; Bildungs-/Schulabschluss **to be qualified**
Young people without qualifications are pushed to the back of the jobs queue.

scholarship Stipendium
I got a full scholarship to Harvard because my grades were so good.

tuition fee Studiengebühr
Tuition fees are very high at many private universities in the US.

undergraduate/graduate Bachelorstudent/Masterstudent; Doktorand
The average age of undergraduates at our university is 21.1 years; for graduates, it is 32.

vocational education/qualification Berufsausbildung/berufliche Qualifikation
A vocational education provides young people with job skills.

 32 *Form word pairs from the words below and use them to complete the sentences.*

vocational • degree • education • distance • tuition • financial • courses • fee • qualifications • learning • higher • aid

1. Joe didn't go to university; he said he couldn't afford the high _____ _____ .

2. Katy's parents were quite poor, so she was really glad she got _____ _____ to go to university.

3. Young people who train to do a particular job, in the car industry for example, get _____ _____ .

4. About 50 per cent of 18-year-olds go on to _____ _____ after they leave school.

5. If you do _____ _____ you will do most of your course online with a few classes at weekends.

6. These days, nurses are trained at university, so _____ _____ in nursing have become very popular.

EDUCATION

LEARNING

to achieve one's potential sein Potenzial ausschöpfen   **achievement** (n.)
A good education helps children to achieve their potential.

to acquire skills Kenntnisse/Fähigkeiten erwerben   **acquisition** (n.)
They've acquired valuable career skills through internships.

to assess s.th. etw. bewerten   **assessment** (n.)
My teacher hasn't assessed my work fairly.

evening class Abendkurs
We went to evening classes to learn Spanish.

examiner Prüfer   **to examine; examination** (n.)
There will be three examiners at the exams next week.

to gain knowledge Wissen erwerben   **knowledgeable** (adj.)
We've gained knowledge of many different subjects this year.

hands-on experience praktische Erfahrung
I think it's good to get hands-on experience and not just classroom learning.

illiterate des Lesens und Schreibens unkundig   **illiteracy** (n.) | ≠ **literate**
Britain has a large number of illiterate adults, according to a new report.

library Bibliothek
I spent the whole afternoon in the library, looking for books.

to pass an exam eine Prüfung bestehen   ≠ **to fail an exam**
People over the age of 75 should have to pass an exam to continue driving.

to revise wiederholen; (für eine Prüfung) lernen   **revision** (n.)
They revised for the exams all weekend.

SCHOOL

(senior) high school (AE)   Oberstufe
My high school offers Spanish and French, but not German.

A levels/Advanced levels (BE)   entspricht Abitur
We are waiting for our A-level results.

assembly   Schulversammlung   **to assemble**
Our school meets for an assembly every morning.

to attend school   die Schule besuchen   **attendance** (n.)
I attended school in London for six years.

? 33 *Complete the sentences with words from these two pages.*

1. Emily _____ new skills when she changed her job.
2. In most industrialised countries, children _____ school until they are 16.
3. While Tom was in China, he _____ a lot of knowledge of Chinese culture.
4. Helen can't go out this evening, she has got to _____ for her maths test.
5. Our school works hard to make sure all our pupils _____ their potential.
6. We will give you the results of your exams as soon as we have _____ your work.
7. Carol didn't enjoy the theory much, but she loved getting _____ experience at the hospital.
8. Because of the war, many children missed school and some were almost _____ .

EDUCATION

boarding school Internat — **to board**
She has been going to boarding school since she was seven.

to bully s.o. jdn. mobben/schikanieren — **bully** (n.)
He bullied one of the smaller children for weeks.

to cheat schummeln; betrügen — **cheat** (n.)
Half the class cheated in the last test.

co-educational/co-ed gemischt — ≠ **single-sex**
Co-educational schools have become the norm in the US.

comprehensive school (BE) Gesamtschule
I enjoy the diversity of my comprehensive school.

compulsory education verbindliche allgemeine Schulbildung; Schulpflicht
Britain's system of compulsory education requires every child to go to school.

to copy abschreiben — **copy** (n.)
She wanted to copy my work, but I didn't let her.

core subject Kernfach
Core subjects include maths and English.

to take a course einen Kurs belegen
What math courses should you take in high school?

coursework Arbeit für die Schule/Universität
She wasn't able to finish her coursework due to illness.

curriculum Lehrplan — **curricular** (adj.)
The state English curriculum is very demanding.

Department for Education (BE)/**Department of Education** (AE)
Bildungsministerium
The Department for Education plans to require children to learn a language.

to drop out of school die Schule abbrechen   **dropout** (n.)
He is getting bad grades and wants to drop out of school.

primary school (BE)/**elementary school** (AE) Grundschule
We have an excellent elementary school in our town.

to be eligible for s.th. Anspruch auf etw. haben   **eligibility** (n.) | ≠ **ineligible**
Children from low-income families are eligible for free school meals.

 34 *Write the English translation in the space provided.*

1. Internat

2. gemischt

3. die Schule abbrechen

4. Schulpflicht

5. Grundschule

6. jdn. mobben/schikanieren

7. Anspruch auf etw. haben

8. Gesamtschule

9. schummeln, betrügen

10. einen Kurs belegen

EDUCATION

entrance exam Aufnahmeprüfung
You will have to take a difficult entrance exam for that school.

exchange student Austauschstudent
Our school welcomes exchange students from around the world.

extra-curricular activity außerunterrichtliche Veranstaltung; Freizeitaktivität
The long school day leaves less time for extra-curricular activities like sports.

to fail an exam durch eine Prüfung fallen   **failure** (n.)
She failed her A-levels but she wants to retake them.

formal education Schulbildung
She never had a formal education: she's self-taught.

freshman/sophomore/junior/senior (AE) Schüler(in) im 1./2./3./4. Jahr der High School oder Student(in) im 1./2./3./4. Jahr des Studiums
There are 382 students in the freshman class this year.

GCSE/General Certificate of Secondary Education (BE)
mittlerer Bildungsabschluss mit 16
One in four pupils study a language at GCSE.

grade (AE) Jahrgang; auch: Note
The whole eighth grade is going on a class trip.

graduation Abschlussfeier   **to graduate; graduate** (n.)
Graduation is in May of this year.

head teacher (BE) Schulleiter(in)
The head teacher is strict, but fair.

independent school (BE) Privatschule; Schule in freier Trägerschaft
Independent schools do not receive money from the government.

infant school (BE) Schule für Kinder zwischen 4 und 7 Jahren
Our infant school gives all children the best possible start for their education.

EDUCATION

junior high school (AE)   Mittelschule
The new junior high school will also include the sixth grade.

junior school (BE)   Schule für Kinder zwischen 7 und 11 Jahren
Our junior school is for boys and girls aged 7 – 11.

to mark s.th.   etw. benoten/korrigieren   **mark** (n.)
He marked history essays all night.

 35 *Solve the puzzle using words from these two pages.*

Across
1. A letter or number that shows the quality of a student's work
2. Adjective for the kind of education you get at school, not at home
3. To correct a student's work
4. You have to pay to go to a school like this.
5. Things you do in your free time, not at school are extra-_ _ _ _ _ _ _ _ _ activities.
6. Adjective that describes a student visiting a school from a foreign country
7. An exam you take to get accepted for a school or university is an _ _ _ _ _ _ _ _ exam.
8. Word for a student in the 4th year of high school
9. Word for a student in the 3rd year of high school
10. An _ _ _ _ _ _ school is for children aged 4 to 7.

Down
1. A celebration of finishing school or university

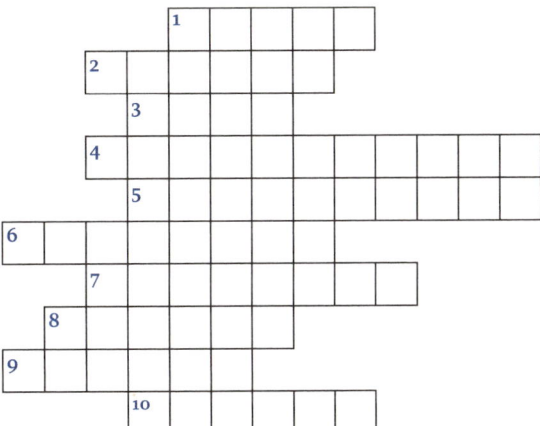

EDUCATION

member of staff Lehrkraft
She was a member of staff at our school, but now she's at a different school.

mock exam Probeklausur
We'll be taking a mock exam to practise for the real exam.

national curriculum zentraler Lehrplan
Experts have helped develop a national curriculum for computer science.

nursery (BE)/**nursery school** (AE) Kindergarten
My three-year-old son goes to nursery school every morning.

Ofsted = Office for Standards in Education (BE) Schulaufsichtsbehörde
Ofsted will be inspecting our school this week.

oral examination mündliche Prüfung
I'm much better at oral examinations than written ones.

to perform a task eine Aufgabe verrichten   **performance** (n.)
Students should perform this task in small groups.

period Schulstunde
Our school day is divided into six periods.

to play truant (BE)/ **to skip school** (AE) die Schule schwänzen   **truancy** (n.)
We used to play truant almost every afternoon.

primary education Grundschulbildung
In their primary education, children learn basic reading and maths skills.

principal (AE) Schulleiter(in)
There will be a new principal in charge of our school next year.

public school exklusive Privatschule (BE); staatliche Schule (AE)
Eton is one of England's oldest public schools.

EDUCATION

to raise standards das Niveau heben
A campaign aims to raise educational standards in Africa's most populous country.

reception (class) (BE) Vorschule
His five-year-old daughter is in the reception class this year.

record Leistung; Bilanz
Her academic record isn't very good.

 36 *Match each word or expression with its translation.*

1. zentraler Lehrplan
2. Schulaufsichtsbehörde (BE)
3. mündliche Prüfung
4. Schulstunde
5. Schulleiter(in) (AE)
6. Vorschule
7. Probeklausur
8. exklusive Privatschule (BE)/ staatliche Schule (AE)
9. die Schule schwänzen
10. Leistung; Bilanz
11. das Niveau heben
12. Kindergarten
13. Grundschulbildung
14. eine Aufgabe verrichten
15. Lehrkraft

a) member of staff
b) mock exam
c) national curriculum
d) nursery (school)
e) Ofsted
f) oral examination
g) to perform a task
h) period
i) primary education
j) to play truant/to skip school
k) principal
l) public school
m) to raise standards
n) reception (class)
o) record

1. ___ 2. ___ 3. ___ 4. ___ 5. ___ 6. ___ 7. ___ 8. ___ 9. ___

10. ___ 11. ___ 12. ___ 13. ___ 14. ___ 15. ___

EDUCATION

report (BE)/**report card** (AE)   Zeugnis
I got an excellent report this year!

reputation   Ruf
Our school has an excellent reputation.

SAT = Scholastic Assessment Test (AE)   Universitätsaufnahmeprüfung
I did well on the math part of the SATs.

secondary education   höhere Schulbildung
Her secondary education ended at the age of 16.

secondary school   weiterführende Schule
State secondary schools have cut the time spent teaching languages to 11- to 14-year-olds.

single-sex   nach Geschlechtern getrennt   ≠ **mixed**
Some people think that girls learn better in single-sex schools.

to sit an exam/**to take a test**   eine Prüfung ablegen; eine Klausur schreiben
I'll be sitting three exams next week and I'm very nervous.

sixth form (BE)   Oberstufe   **sixth-former** (n.)
I'll be starting the sixth form after the summer holidays.

special educational needs   sonderpädagogischer Förderbedarf
This school also admits students with special educational needs.

subject   Unterrichtsfach
My favourite subject is biology.

supply teacher (BE)/**substitute teacher** (AE)   Vertretungslehrer(in)
We had a supply teacher last week because Mrs Jones was ill.

EDUCATION

 37 Use words from the 'education' section to complete the crossword. Put the letters in the blue squares in the correct order to find a famous university.

Across
3. Opposite of 'pass'
7. See 13 across
9. To do something dishonest to help you in an exam
10. This is where you go to borrow books.
11. Unable to read and write
12. If you get this, your studies at university are paid for.
13. and 7 across Money you pay for studying at a university
14. A school that is just for boys or girls is single-_ _ _.

Down
1. To study something as your main subject (AE)
2. Subjects like literature and history
4. Information on the quality of your work, made by a teacher
5. A qualification you get from a university
6. To be mean to someone and hurt them
8. To leave school before you have got qualifications (two words)

University: ___ ___ ___ ___ ___ ___ ___ ___ ___

GOVERNMENT, LAW & POLITICS
4 CIVIL RIGHTS

to be involved in s.th.

in etw. involviert sein; an etw. beteiligt sein   **involvement** (n.)

Maya Angelou became involved with the civil rights movement in the 1960s.

---

civil disobedience ziviler Ungehorsam

A civil disobedience movement resulted in the departure of the British from India.

---

civil liberties bürgerliche Freiheiten

Civil liberties activists protested the unfair laws.

---

civil rights movement Bürgerrechtsbewegung

In 1964, Martin Luther King was the leader of America's civil rights movement.

---

the Deep South der tiefe Süden

The Deep South was a black and white world in 1965.

---

demonstration Demonstration   **to demonstrate; demonstrator** (n.)

Some social activists have organised demonstrations to protest against the film.

---

equality Gleichberechtigung   **equal** (adj.) | ≠ **inequality**

We live in an era of equality, with women in the same roles as men.

---

freedom Freiheit   **to free; free** (adj.)

America has a tradition of tolerance and religious freedom.

---

justice Gerechtigkeit   **just** (adj.); **justly** (adv.) | ≠ **injustice**

We are hoping for justice from the British government.

---

oppression Unterdrückung   **to oppress; oppressor** (n.); **oppressive** (adj.)

For African Americans, the Confederacy is a symbol of racial oppression.

---

prejudice Vorurteil   **prejudiced** (adj.)

Gay activists say that much prejudice remains in India.

GOVERNMENT, LAW & POLITICS

to protest against s.th. gegen etw. protestieren   **protest** (n.); **protestor** (n.)
Indigenous people protested against conditions on Indian reservations.

racial tension Rassenspannungen   **race** (n.); **racist** (n.); **tense** (adj.)
Racial tensions are a powerful problem in South Africa.

rally Kundgebung   **to rally**
People have held rallies in a show of unity.

to refuse s. weigern   **refusal** (n.)
Rosa Parks refused to give up her seat to a white man on a bus in 1955.

38 *Complete each sentence with a word from the same family as the word in brackets.*

1. Most of the _____ who took part in the march were peaceful. (to demonstrate)

2. The Declaration of Independence states that all men were created _____ . (equality)

3. After years in prison, Mandela finally walked _____ . (freedom)

4. Black South Africans regarded Afrikaans as the language of the _____ . (oppression)

5. The football players were criticised for their _____ to stand for the national anthem. (to refuse)

6. The judge was known for his strict but _____ decisions. (justice)

7. As an African American, Robert sometimes experienced _____ at work. (prejudiced)

8. He was sent to prison because of his _____ in drug dealing. (to involve)

GOVERNMENT, LAW & POLITICS

segregation Rassentrennung   to segregate; segregated (adj.) | ≠ desegregation
The Civil Rights and Voting Rights Acts made segregation illegal.

to struggle against s.th.   gegen etw. kämpfen   struggle (n.)
Blacks in South Africa struggled against apartheid for years.

CRIME

to abuse s.o. jdn. missbrauchen   abuser (n.); abuse (n.); abusive (adj.)
It is difficult for boys to talk about being sexually abused.

accident Unfall   accidental (adj.)
Around 130,000 people died in road accidents in India last year.

to accuse s.o. jdn. beschuldigen   accusation (n.); accuser (n.)
The three men were accused of planning to bomb the apartments.

to acquit s.o. (of s.th.) jdn. (von etw.) freisprechen   acquittal (n.)
He was acquitted of killing the teenager.

to admit (to) s.th. etw. zugeben   admission (n.)
She admitted marrying her fifth husband without divorcing the previous four.

allegation Vorwurf   to allege; alleged (adj.); allegedly (adv.)
The president apologized following allegations of sexism.

to arrest s.o. jdn. verhaften   arrest (n.)
The police say that more than 1,200 people have been arrested.

assassination Mordanschlag   to assassinate; assassin (n.)
Pierre Laporte's killing was the only assassination of a Canadian political figure in the 20th century.

to assault angreifen   assault (n.); assailant (n.)
Police are searching for a teen who assaulted and killed a man.

GOVERNMENT, LAW & POLITICS

lawyer/attorney (AE) Anwalt/Anwältin
You have the right to a lawyer.

bombing Bombenanschlag **to bomb**
The group carried out a 1988 bombing in Northern Ireland.

to break a law ein Gesetz brechen
He broke the law twice, and I arrested him both times.

bribe Bestechungsgeld/-mittel **to bribe (s.o.); bribery** (n.)
The bribes are often something as simple as fresh apples or bananas.

 39 Complete the grid with words from the word families. A dash (–) means you don't have to find a word. If there are two nouns, write down both.

noun	verb	adjective
	to abuse	
accident	–	
	to admit	–
allegation		
	to assassinate	–
		segregated
acquittal		–
bribery		–
	to accuse	–

GOVERNMENT, LAW & POLITICS

burglary Einbruch   **to burgle** (BE)/**burglarize** (AE); **burglar** (n.)
Greater security in homes means that it is more difficult to carry out burglaries.

capital punishment Todesstrafe   = **death penalty**
Alaska has removed capital punishment from its laws.

to charge s.o. with a crime jdn. eines Verbrechens beschuldigen   **charge** (n.)
The boys had not been charged with any crime.

child abuse Kindesmisshandlung   **to abuse; abuser** (n.); **abusive** (adj.)
Hitting children in schools is child abuse.

to commit a crime ein Verbrechen begehen
The crimes were committed between 1996 and 2002.

to do community service gemeinnützige Arbeit/Sozialstunden leisten   **to serve**
He was made to do 300 hours of community service as punishment.

to confess gestehen   **confession** (n.)
She confessed to the crime after the police questioned her.

to convict s.o. jdn. verurteilen   **conviction** (n.)
She was convicted of hiring three men to kill her husband.

criminal Verbrecher(in)   **crime** (n.); **criminal** (adj.)
The criminals were paid 25,000 rupees to break into temples.

criminal law Strafgesetz/-recht
Under Canadian criminal law it is not illegal to kill dogs using a gun.

criminal offence (BE)/**offense** (AE) Straftat   **to offend; offensive** (adj.)
When I was young, it was a criminal offense to be homosexual.

custodial sentence (BE) Haftstrafe   **custody** (n.)
The crime led to a custodial sentence.

GOVERNMENT, LAW & POLITICS

cyberbullying Cybermobbing   **to bully s.o.**
Cyberbullying is a new problem facing some of our teenagers.

to defend oneself s. verteidigen   **defence** (n.) (BE)/**defense** (n.) (AE)
If she takes me to court, I will be defending myself.

defendant Angeklagte(r)   **to defend**
The defendant said that he had mistakenly shot his girlfriend.

40 *Complete the sentences with words and expressions from these two pages.*

1. I disagree with _____ ; it is never right to kill another human being, even if he or she has _____ a terrible crime.

2. After hours of questioning, the suspect _____ to the crime.

3. We had a _____ yesterday, and all the money we had in the house was stolen.

4. The police had enough evidence, so he was _____ with the murder of his son.

5. The teenager had stolen a pair of sneakers and was ordered to do 100 hours of _____ service.

6. The two men were _____ of robbery and assault and sent to prison.

7. The six-year old was much too thin and had a broken arm: it was a clear case of child _____ .

8. The _____ said that he was not guilty.

83

GOVERNMENT, LAW & POLITICS

delinquent straffällig (bes. Jugendliche) **delinquent** (n.); **delinquency** (n.)
Holden Caulfield is the delinquent antihero of The Catcher in the Rye.

domestic violence häusliche Gewalt **violent** (adj.)
Eighty-five per cent of the victims of domestic violence are women.

to enforce a law ein Gesetz durchsetzen **enforcement** (n.)
You need laws, and you need to enforce them.

espionage Spionage **to spy; spy** (n.)
The network was infected with software that permitted an espionage attack.

evidence Beweis(e)
The group presented its evidence to the commission yesterday.

execution Hinrichtung **to execute (s.o); executioner** (n.)
Five countries are responsible for almost all the state executions carried out in the past year.

to fall victim to s.o./s.th. Opfer von jdm./etw. werden
Tourists have not fallen victim to crime here.

fine Geldstrafe **to fine s.o.**
She was ordered to pay a $3,000 fine.

firearm Schusswaffe
Firearms are not allowed in government buildings.

forgery Fälschung **to forge; forger** (n.)
The gallery closed during a forgery scandal.

fraud Betrug **fraudulent** (adj.)
Internet fraud costs billions of pounds a year.

to gain access to s.th. Zugang zu etw. erlangen **to access**
Hackers gained access to the bank's computer system.

GOVERNMENT, LAW & POLITICS

guilty schuldig   **guilt** (n.) | ≠ **innocent**
Several teenagers were found guilty of cheating in last summer's exams.

gun control Reglementierung von Waffenbesitz
There have been increasing calls for more gun control in the U.S.

gun ownership Waffenbesitz
Montana has one of the country's highest rates of gun ownership.

? 41 *Use the parts of words below to make words that replace the question marks.*

cution • force • vio • cess • dence • for • arm • gery • evi • exe • lence • en • ac • fire

1. The painting looked genuine, but an expert said it was only a very good ? .

2. After the murder, the police searched the house for ? .

3. Politicians create laws, but police officers ? them.

4. In the UK, it is illegal to carry a ? ; even police officers don't carry guns.

5. The prisoner stood blindfolded against a wall, waiting for his ? .

6. The police saw that the woman had been beaten; it was a case of domestic ? .

7. The hacker gained ? to passwords, bank accounts and personal information.

Use the letters in the blue squares to find the word that means 'not guilty'.

___ ___ ___ ___ ___ ___ ___ ___

GOVERNMENT, LAW & POLITICS

to hack into a system ein System hacken **hacker** (n.)
There are 1,000 attempts to hack into British Telecom's computer system every day.

to harass s.o. jdn. belästigen **harassment** (n.); **harasser** (n.)
The new law punishes men who harass women.

to hijack entführen **hijacking** (n.)
Two terrorists hijacked the plane.

homicide Tötungsdelikt **homicidal** (adj.)
The police department is working to solve the homicides.

imprisonment Inhaftierung **to imprison**
He was freed after 12 days' imprisonment.

innocent unschuldig **innocence** | ≠ **guilty**
Often it is innocent people who suffer.

investigation Untersuchung; Ermittlung **to investigate; investigator** (n.)
The investigation of the school found no wrongdoing.

jail/prison Gefängnis **prisoner** (n.)
He left jail last summer after serving a year for robbery.

judge Richter(in) **to judge; judg(e)ment** (n.)
The judge took about three hours to reach his decision.

to kidnap s.o. jdn. entführen **kidnapper** (n.); **kidnapping** (n.)
Paul Rose kidnapped minister of labour Pierre Laporte in 1970.

lethal injection Todesspritze **to inject**
Nebraska switched from the electric chair to lethal injections in 2008.

manslaughter Totschlag
The police officer was charged with manslaughter in the death of a black man.

GOVERNMENT, LAW & POLITICS

to mug s.o. jdn. auf offener Straße ausrauben **mugger** (n.); **mugging** (n.)
He was mugged in the park.

to murder s.o. jdn. ermorden **murder** (n.); **murderer** (n.); **murderous** (adj.)
More people are murdered in Chicago than anywhere else in the US.

offence (BE)/**offense** (AE) Straftat **offender** (n.)
Immigrants convicted of serious criminal offences could be barred from citizenship.

42 *Complete the sentences with words from these two pages that match the definitions in brackets.*

1. Katy was _____ while walking home from the bus stop. (robbed in the street)

2. The police said it was definitely a case of _____, either murder or manslaughter. (the killing of another person)

3. The man told police that he had an alibi and that he was _____. (not guilty)

4. The murderer was sentenced to 15 years _____. (the state of being in prison)

5. Jane complained to the manager that her co-worker was _____ her. (to annoy and upset s.o. repeatedly)

6. The electric chair is no longer used in the US; it has been replaced by the _____. (drugs injected to cause death)

7. The police are still carrying out their _____ of the attack and can't say yet whether it was an act of terrorism. (examination of a crime)

8. As it was his first _____, the judge let him off with a fine. (crime)

GOVERNMENT, LAW & POLITICS

penalty Strafe **to penalize/penalise** (BE)
The maximum penalty is three months in prison.

piracy Piraterie **pirate** (n.)
Record companies' profits have been cut by piracy.

to place s.o. under house arrest jdn. unter Hausarrest stellen
Aung San Suu Kyi was placed under house arrest in 1989.

to plead guilty s. schuldig bekennen **plea** (n.)
He pleaded guilty to ten crimes.

probation Bewährung **probation officer** (n.); **probationary** (adj.)
He was sentenced to a year of probation.

prosecutor/prosecuting attorney (AE) Staatsanwalt/-anwältin
The prosecutor has requested that the trial take place behind closed doors.

to prove s.o.'s innocence jds. Unschuld beweisen **innocent** (adj.) | ≠ **guilt**
The DNA test proved her innocence in 1993.

to put s.o. on trial jdn. vor Gericht bringen
The men were put on trial three years after the crime.

rape Vergewaltigung **to rape** (s.o.); **rapist** (n.)
Women in the military face sexual discrimination and rape.

to reduce a sentence eine Strafe mildern
Her six-year sentence was later reduced.

to release s.o. from prison jdn. aus dem Gefängnis entlassen **release** (n.)
He was released from prison after 90 days.

rifle Gewehr
Lee Harvey Oswald killed President John F Kennedy with a $12 rifle.

GOVERNMENT, LAW & POLITICS

security Sicherheit **to secure; secure** (adj.)
Internet security is seriously in danger.

to seize s.th. etw. beschlagnahmen **seizure** (n.)
Exotic animals are often seized at airports.

to sentence s.o. to death jdn. zum Tode verurteilen
The two men were arrested and later sentenced to death.

? 43 *Write the English word or expression in the space provided.*

1. Vergewaltigung _____

2. s. schuldig bekennen _____

3. etw. beschlagnahmen _____

4. jdn. zum Tode verurteilen _____

5. Strafe _____

6. Bewährung _____

7. jdn. vor Gericht bringen _____

8. jds. Unschuld beweisen _____

9. jdn. aus dem Gefängnis entlassen _____

10. Staatsanwalt _____

GOVERNMENT, LAW & POLITICS

to serve a sentence eine Strafe absitzen
They served only light sentences for their crimes.

---

to smuggle s.th. etw. schmuggeln   **smuggler** (n.)
She was caught trying to smuggle 27kg of gold into the country.

---

solitary confinement Einzelhaft   **to confine**
The prisoner spent a year in solitary confinement.

---

stimulant Aufputschmittel   **to stimulate**
Stimulants can cause hallucinations when taken in high doses.

---

suspect Verdächtiger   **to suspect; suspicious** (adj.)
The police said they were close to finding one suspect.

---

to take s.o. hostage jdn. als Geisel nehmen   **hostage** (n.); **hostage-taker** (n.)
The hostages were taken by a terrorist group.

---

to testify aussagen   **testimony** (n.)
She testified against her boyfriend in court.

---

theft Diebstahl   **thief** (n.)
Theft of religious art is a big problem in India.

---

threat Gefahr; Bedrohung   **to threaten**
The biggest online threat comes from hackers in foreign states such as Russia.

---

trafficking illegaler Handel   **to traffic**
Police are questioning celebrities in connection with drug trafficking and abuse.

---

trial Gerichtsverfahren
The trial will focus attention on the religious artworks stolen from India's temples.

---

victim Opfer   **to victimize/to victimise** (BE); **victimization** (n.)
Most victims of stalkers are women.

90

GOVERNMENT, LAW & POLITICS

weapon Waffe
Children as young as seven are used by gangs to carry weapons.

POLITICS

to abolish abschaffen   **abolition** (n.)
Most countries have abolished the death penalty.

accession Beitritt   **to accede**
An independent Scotland would have to join the EU as a new accession state.

? 44 *Use words and expressions from these two pages to replace the underlined words in the sentences.*

1. The worst part of prison was the time in his cell without any contact to others.

2. The police said the person they thought had committed the crime was a 40-year-old Londoner.

3. The gang was involved in illegally selling guns and knives.

4. The bank robbers said they would only let the people they had taken as security go if they were allowed to leave with the money.

5. She gave evidence in court and said she saw her boss stealing the money.

6. After the accident, the people who were hurt were taken to hospital.

7. He was arrested for illegally dealing with drugs.

8. After Sandra had done her time in prison she promised herself she would never break the law again.

GOVERNMENT, LAW & POLITICS

to advocate s.th. etw. befürworten **advocacy** (n.); **advocate** (n.)
The organisation advocates reduced immigration.

affairs Angelegenheiten
She has strong views about world affairs.

agreement Abkommen **to agree**
The EU-Canada trade agreement took four years to negotiate.

ally Verbündete(r) **to ally**
After World War II, Germany was occupied by the allies.

ambassador Botschafter(in)
The Syrian ambassador was invited, and then uninvited.

to amend ändern **amendment** (n.)
The Department for Education said the government had no plans to amend the law.

to appoint s.o. jdn. einsetzen/ernennen **appointment** (n.)
The experts were appointed by the president.

to approve s.th. etw. genehmigen/billigen **approval** (n.)
Congress approved the law this week.

ballot Wahlzettel
We have the right to change our national government through the power of the ballot.

ballot box Wahlurne
In the privacy of the ballot box, the people made a public statement.

to ban s.th. etw. verbieten **ban** (n.) | ≠ **to allow**
The Taleban banned kite-flying as un-Islamic.

GOVERNMENT, LAW & POLITICS

to be eligible to vote wahlberechtigt sein   **eligibility** (n.)
About 3.5 million Britons will be eligible to vote for the first time in May.

bill Gesetzesvorlage
The president said that signing the bill sent a clear message.

to cast a vote eine Stimme abgeben
More than 550 million votes were cast in the general election.

checks and balances Gewaltenteilung
James Madison laid out his theory of checks and balances in the Constitution.

 45 *Find the correct endings to the sentences.*

1. A diplomat who represents a state in a foreign country is
2. The container voters put their voting papers in is
3. If you make small changes to a law to improve it you
4. A state which cooperates with another state is
5. If politicians publicly support a law or a policy, they
6. If a president names a person to do an important job, he
7. If lawmakers officially accept and agree with a law, they
8. If you forbid something, especially something harmful, you
9. If you are legally allowed to do something you are
10. A system that makes sure power is not concentrated in one person or group is a system of

a) checks and balances.
b) an ambassador.
c) advocate it.
d) a ballot box.
e) amend it.
f) appoints them.
g) ban it.
h) approve it.
i) eligible to do it.
j) an ally.

1. ____ 2. ____ 3. ____ 4. ____ 5. ____ 6. ____ 7. ____

8. ____ 9. ____ 10. ____

93

GOVERNMENT, LAW & POLITICS

citizen Staatsbürger(in) **citizenship** (n.)
You have to be able to speak English before becoming a citizen.

to come into force in Kraft treten
The new law came into force on 1 January.

to come into/to power/take power an die Macht kommen
Labour came to power in 1997.

to be committed to s.th. s. für etw. engagieren/verpflichten **commitment** (n.)
We were very committed to our work.

consent Zustimmung **to consent**
The Kremlin announced Russia's consent to the agreement.

constituent Wähler(in) (eines Wahlkreises) **constituency** (n.)
Scottish and Welsh MPs are able to vote on English matters which will not affect their constituents.

defence (BE)/**defense** (AE) Verteidigung
Germany and Japan both spend a significant amount on defence.

to delay s.th. etw. verschieben **delay** (n.)
A full vote may be delayed until after the November election.

to deliver/give a speech eine Rede halten
Dr Martin Luther King delivered his 'I have a dream' speech in 1963.

duty Pflicht **dutiful** (adj.)
Most adults believe that it is their duty to vote.

to elect s.o. jdn. wählen **election** (n.)
Nelson Mandela was South Africa's first democratically elected president.

election campaign Wahlkampf **to campaign**
The candidate showed his coolness under fire during the election campaign.

GOVERNMENT, LAW & POLITICS

electorate Wählerschaft **to elect; election** (n.)
Black, Hispanic and Asian voters made up nearly a quarter of the electorate.

to eliminate s.th. etw. abschaffen **elimination** (n.)
The candidate wants to eliminate income tax.

to enshrine s.th. in law/the Constitution
etw. im Gesetz/in der Verfassung verankern
A right to education is enshrined in the constitutions of more than 140 countries.

 46 Solve the puzzle with words from these two pages.

Across
1. Protection against or reaction to an attack
3. You can give a speech or you can _ _ _ _ _ _ _ it.
4. Agreement to do something or allow something to happen
5. A person who is legally recognised as having full rights in a state
6. A person who lives in an electoral district
7. If a law comes into _ _ _ _ _ it starts to be effective.
8. To protect an idea, right or tradition by including it in law or the constitution
9. A series of activities aimed at getting a candidate or party elected
10. A responsibility
11. To do something later than planned

Down
2. All the people who are allowed to vote in a state or area

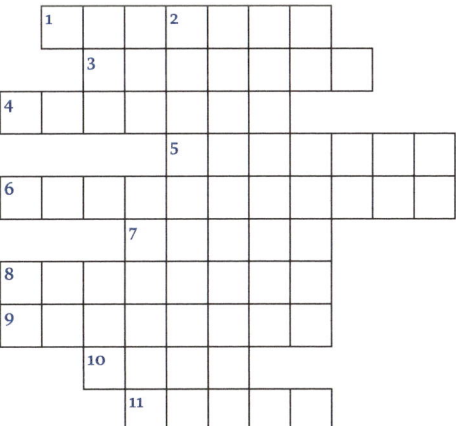

GOVERNMENT, LAW & POLITICS

to establish s.th. etw. etablieren/gründen · **establishment** (n.)
The Bank of England was established to lend to the government.

to expand s.th. etw. erweitern · **expansion** (n.)
George Washington was celebrated for expanding the Union.

foreign policy Außenpolitik
President Obama made a series of dramatic foreign policy breaks with George Bush.

to found s.th. etw. gründen · **founder** (n.); **foundation** (n.)
The world's first Green Party was founded in 1972.

to fund s.th. etw. finanzieren · **fund** (n.); **funding** (n.)
Roosevelt's New Deal created jobs through public projects funded by borrowing.

to govern regieren · **government** (n.)
The ANC has governed South Africa for most of my life.

to have/achieve an overall majority eine absolute Mehrheit haben/erreichen
The party did not achieve an overall majority in the last election.

to have a say (in s.th.) Mitspracherecht (bei etw.) haben
Scottish voters want to have a say before Britain leaves the EU.

head of state Staatsoberhaupt
The two countries have both dropped the Queen as head of state.

to head s.th. etw. leiten · **head** (n.)
He heads the state's art and culture department.

to hold a general election eine allgemeine Wahl abhalten
Britain will hold a general election on May 7.

to hold an election eine Wahl abhalten · **to elect**
She asked the prime minister to hold an election immediately.

GOVERNMENT, LAW & POLITICS

to **impeach** wegen Amtsvergehen anklagen   **impeachment** (n.)
She has said that the president should be impeached.

to **impose/lift sanctions** Sanktionen verhängen/aufheben
New sanctions have been imposed against North Korea.

to **influence** beeinflussen   **influence** (n.); **influential** (adj.)
No one set of beliefs has more right to influence the public debate than any other.

47 *Put the letters in brackets in the correct order to find the words that complete the sentences.*

1. The party has not got an _____, so they will have to form a coalition with one of the other parties. (**vaolelr, yraimotj**)

2. If the investigation finds that the president has cooperated with Russia, lawmakers could decide to _____ him. (**hipamec**)

3. The Queen does not _____ Britain, but she has an important ceremonial role. (**ngevor**)

4. The US has decided to _____ sanctions on Iran, which will hit the country's oil exports, shipping and banks. (**eopism**)

5. The Defense Secretary resigned because he disagreed with the president's _____, especially in the Middle East. (**iofnerg, cpyoil**)

6. The United Nations was officially _____ on October 24, 1945. (**aedehbssilt**)

7. The prime minister said she was considering holding an early _____. (**aglerne, ncetlieo**)

GOVERNMENT, LAW & POLITICS

to intervene eingreifen   **intervention** (n.)
The government intervened to stop the strike.

landslide victory Erdrutschsieg
Republicans took control of the House of Representatives in a landslide victory.

to launch s.th. etw. einführen; etw. starten; etw. lancieren   **launch** (n.)
He launched his candidacy two months ago.

legislation Gesetzgebung; Gesetze **to legislate; legislature** (n.); **legislative** (adj.)
Some parties think the legislation does not go far enough.

member state Mitgliedsstaat
Of the 28 EU member states, six do not belong to the Schengen zone.

opponent Gegner(in)   **to oppose; opposition** (n.)
Donald Trump is an opponent of free-trade deals.

to pass a law ein Gesetz verabschieden
The state's anti-immigration law was passed in 2010.

to pledge to do s.th. s. verpflichten etw. zu tun   **pledge** (n.)
The president has pledged to find a cure for the disease.

policy Politik
Others plan to work on changing government food policy.

politician Politiker(in)
Kenyan politicians are among the highest paid in the world.

polling station Wahllokal
You can vote at a polling station near your home.

population Bevölkerung   **to populate; populous** (adj.)
About 60% of Africa's population is aged under 25.

GOVERNMENT, LAW & POLITICS

to promote s.th. etw. fördern **promotion** (n.)
The organisation works to promote democracy around the world.

the public das Volk; die Öffentlichkeit
The Tories are not quite sure why the public has not learned to love them yet.

to ratify a treaty einen Vertrag ratifizieren **ratification** (n.)
All member states have to ratify the treaty.

48 *Use words and expressions from these two pages to replace the underlined words in the sentences.*

1. The Paris agreement was <u>signed and confirmed</u> by most of the countries in the world. _____

2. The <u>places where people cast their votes</u> were kept open until 10 p.m. _____

3. President Trump <u>promised</u> to build a wall along the border with Mexico. _____

4. The election resulted in a <u>very big</u> victory for the Republicans. _____

5. There were protests against fracking, and the Green Party candidate was one of the <u>people who were against it</u>. _____

6. Congress passed <u>laws</u> that restricted immigration and set quotas. _____

7. The EU has 28 <u>countries belonging to it</u>, including the UK, which is about to leave. _____

8. The police <u>got involved</u> to prevent the attack on peaceful demonstrators. _____

99

GOVERNMENT, LAW & POLITICS

to represent s.o. jdn. vertreten **representation** (n.); **representative** (n.)
The group represents the country's Muslims.

to resign zurücktreten **resignation** (n.)
Kevin Rudd resigned as Australia's foreign minister during a visit to Washington.

to respond to s.th. auf etw. reagieren **response** (n.); **responsive** (adj.)
The government has begun to respond to the crisis.

to serve a term eine Amtszeit durchlaufen
The president can only serve for two terms.

to sign a treaty einen Vertrag unterschreiben **signature** (n.)
He said his nation had never signed a treaty with the government.

social security soziale Sicherung (BE)/Rentenversicherung (AE)
I've been paying money into Social Security for the last 40 years.

successor Nachfolger(in) **to succeed (s.o.)**
His successor will be elected at a special congress in December.

supreme court oberstes Gericht
The case went all the way to the US Supreme Court.

to swear an oath einen Eid ablegen
The new president swears an oath of office.

to swear s.o. in jdn. vereidigen
The U.S. president is usually sworn in by the Chief Justice of the Supreme Court.

tax Steuer **to tax; taxation** (n.); **taxpayer** (n.)
Last year, 44 percent of Americans paid no federal income tax.

terrorist attack Terroranschlag
He wants to end Pakistani support for terrorist attacks on India.

GOVERNMENT, LAW & POLITICS

victory Sieg
The Civil War was a victory for freedom.

victor (n.); **victorious** (adj.)

to **vote against** s.th. gegen etw. stimmen
He was one of 36 Republicans who voted against the bill.

vote (n.); **voter** (n.)

voter Wähler(in)
The economy is important to Republican voters in Florida.

❓ 49 Write the English word or expression in the space provided.

1. soziale Sicherung   _____

2. oberstes Gericht   _____

3. einen Vertrag unterschreiben   _____

4. jdn. vertreten   _____

5. Steuer   _____

6. zurücktreten   _____

7. Nachfolger   _____

8. einen Eid ablegen   _____

9. jdn. vereidigen   _____

10. auf etw. reagieren   _____

GOVERNMENT, LAW & POLITICS

polling (BE)/ voting (AE) booth Wahlkabine
Only one voter at a time is allowed to enter a polling booth.

to withdraw zurückziehen   withdrawal (n.)
The plans have been withdrawn following opposition.

POLITICS UK

by-election Nachwahl
The government is facing a by-election this weekend.

Chancellor of the Exchequer (BE) Finanzminister(in)
Alistair Darling was Chancellor of the Exchequer in the last Labour government.

constitutional monarchy
konstitutionelle Monarchie   constitution (n.); monarch (n.)
Every constitutional monarchy that is successful keeps the monarch out of politics.

first-past-the-post system Mehrheitswahlrecht
The UK uses a first-past-the-post voting system.

foreign affairs Außenpolitik
The new prime minister is not greatly interested in foreign affairs.

foreign secretary Außenminister(in)
The foreign secretary wanted a deal to help her country's relationship with Spain.

to form a government eine Regierung bilden
The party that gains most seats usually forms the government.

home secretary Innenminister(in)
Theresa May was home secretary before becoming prime minister.

House of Commons Unterhaus
There are now 187 women in the House of Commons.

GOVERNMENT, LAW & POLITICS

House of Lords Oberhaus
The House of Lords has over 800 members.

MP/Member of Parliament Parlamentsabgeordnete(r)
Eighty-one of the MPs supported the referendum.

politically impartial/neutral politisch neutral ≠ **biased**
The Queen is politically impartial.

speaker Vorsitzende(r) des Unterhauses
The Speaker controls the House of Commons and decides who speaks and when.

 50 *Match each word or expression with its translation.*

1. Außenpolitik
2. Oberhaus
3. Parlamentsabgeordnete(r)
4. Mehrheitswahlrecht
5. eine Regierung bilden
6. Wahlkabine
7. konstitutionelle Monarchie
8. Nachwahl
9. politisch neutral
10. Innenminister(in)
11. Vorsitzende(r) des Unterhauses
12. zurückziehen
13. Unterhaus
14. Außenminister(in)
15. Finanzminister(in)

a) voting/polling booth
b) to withdraw
c) by-election
d) Chancellor of the Exchequer
e) constitutional monarchy
f) first-past-the-post system
g) foreign affairs
h) foreign secretary
i) to form a government
j) politically impartial/neutral
k) home secretary
l) House of Commons
m) speaker
n) MP/Member of Parliament
o) House of Lords

1. ___ 2. ___ 3. ___ 4. ___ 5. ___ 6. ___ 7. ___ 8. ___ 9. ___
10. ___ 11. ___ 12. ___ 13. ___ 14. ___ 15. ___

103

GOVERNMENT, LAW & POLITICS

POLITICS USA

administration Regierung
The rules were blocked by the Bush administration.

Attorney General Justizminister(in)
Loretta E. Lynch was the first African-American woman to be Attorney General.

caucus Vorversammlung von Wählern zur Ernennung eines Kandidaten
Sixteen American states hold caucuses to choose a presidential candidate.

chamber Kammer
A Republican-dominated chamber was elected last month.

commander-in-chief Oberbefehlshaber(in)
The U.S. president acts as commander-in-chief of the military.

Congress Kongress   **congressman/-woman** (n.)
The U.S. Congress is made up of the Senate and the House of Representatives.

constitution Verfassung   **constitutional** (adj.)
Children born in the U.S. are American citizens under the constitution.

convention Parteitag   **to convene**
'Super delegates' can vote for the candidate of their choice at the July convention.

Declaration of Independence Unabhängigkeitserklärung   **to declare**
Thomas Jefferson was the main author of the Declaration of Independence.

to declare s.th. unconstitutional etw. für verfassungswidrig erklären
The new law was declared unconstitutional.

delegate Delegierte(r)   **delegation** (n.)
Each of the candidates already has the votes of more than 150 delegates.

GOVERNMENT, LAW & POLITICS

electoral college Gremium der Wahlmänner und Wahlfrauen
Two hundred seventy electoral college votes are needed to win the presidency.

executive branch Exekutive
The president is the head of the executive branch of the U.S. government.

governor Gouverneur(in)
Arnold Schwarzenegger was the governor of California from 2003 until 2011.

House of Representatives Repräsentantenhaus
The House of Representatives has no more than 435 members.

 51 *Find the correct endings to the sentences.*

1. The US president is the head of the military; he is the
2. People at party conventions who vote for a candidate are
3. In the US, the government is often called the
4. The group of people made up of representatives from each state that elects the president is the
5. In the US the minister of justice is known as the
6. A big party meeting to choose a presidential candidate is a
7. The lower chamber of Congress is the
8. The document that announced the separation from Britain was the

a) House of Representatives.
b) Declaration of Independence.
c) electoral college.
d) Attorney General.
e) administration.
f) delegates.
g) convention.
h) commander-in-chief.

1. _____ 2. _____ 3. _____ 4. _____ 5. _____ 6. _____ 7. _____ 8. _____

105

GOVERNMENT, LAW & POLITICS

to **inaugurate** s.o. jdn. in ein Amt einführen   **inauguration** (n.); **inaugural** (adj.)
The new president will be inaugurated on January 20.

judicial branch Judikative   **judiciary** (n.)
The judicial branch of the U.S. government makes decisions about laws.

legislative branch Legislative   **to legislate; legislator** (n.); **legislation** (n.)
The legislative branch of the U.S. government makes federal laws.

nominee/candidate Kandidat(in)   **to nominate**
Mitt Romney was the Republican presidential nominee in 2012.

primary Vorwahl
Most states hold primaries to choose a candidate for the presidential election.

to **run for president** für das Präsidentenamt kandidieren
I haven't decided yet whether I will run for president.

running mate Kandidat(in) für die Vizepräsidentschaft
Each presidential candidate chooses a running mate, who becomes vice-president if they win.

Secretary of Defense Verteidigungsminister(in)
The secretary of defense said that all ground combat positions are open to women.

Secretary of State Außenminister(in)
The Secretary of State is in charge of United States foreign affairs.

Secretary of the Interior Innenminister(in)
The Secretary of the Interior announced new rules about managing the river.

Senate Senat   **senator** (n.)
The U.S. Senate is made up of two senators from each state.

to **threaten** androhen   **threat** (n.)
North Korea has threatened war against the U.S.

GOVERNMENT, LAW & POLITICS

to uphold s.th. etw. aufrechterhalten; etw. bestätigen
The law was upheld by the Supreme Court.

to veto a bill sein Veto gegen einen Gesetzentwurf einlegen   **veto** (n.)
The governor vetoed the bill.

vice-president Vizepräsident(in)
The vice-president is elected together with the president.

? 52 *Use the parts of words below to make words that replace the question marks.*

icial • up • nee • legis • pri • sec • nomi • inaugur • jud • hold • mary • lative • ation • retary

1. Congress is the ? branch of the US government.

2. In the US, the ? of State is the country's top diplomat.

3. The ? branch of government is made up of judges and courts.

4. The president said that it was important to ? the freedom of the press.

5. Election year started for the candidates with the first ? , in New Hampshire.

6. The delegates at the Republican Convention cheered the presidential ? .

7. At the ? , the U.S. president takes the oath of office.

Find an important American document written in 1787.

___ ___ ___ ___ ___ ___ ___ ___ ___ ___ ___ ___

GOVERNMENT, LAW & POLITICS

WAR AND PEACE

act of war kriegerische Handlung
The president called the murders an act of war.

armed forces Streitkräfte
The Pentagon has broadened the role of women serving in the US armed forces.

to bear arms Waffen tragen **to arm**
The US Constitution protects the right 'to keep and bear arms'.

casualty (Todes-)Opfer
There were many casualties on the English side.

ceasefire Waffenruhe **to cease**
The three leaders agreed on a ceasefire.

chemical weapon chemische Waffe
Chemical weapons have again been used in Syria.

civil war Bürgerkrieg
The Civil War took as many lives as all America's other wars combined.

civilian Zivilist **civilian** (adj.)
At least 25,000 civilians died in bombings in Dresden.

to commit atrocities Gräueltaten begehen **atrocious** (adj.)
The rebels committed mass atrocities in Sierra Leone.

conscription (BE)/**draft** (AE) Wehrpflicht
The country has ended conscription and created a smaller, more professional army.

to declare war on s.o. jdm. den Krieg erklären **declaration** (n.)
Britain declared war on Germany in August 1914.

GOVERNMENT, LAW & POLITICS

defeat Niederlage   **to defeat | ≠ victory**
Lincoln led the defeat of the Confederate states in the American Civil War.

disarmament Abrüstung   **to disarm**
The 1998 Good Friday agreement led to the IRA's disarmament in 2005.

front line Front(linie)
The US does not allow women to serve on the front line.

to go to/wage war Krieg führen
The president said that the US was waging war on extremists.

? 53 *Complete the sentences with words and expressions from these two pages.*

1. Today, women serve alongside men in the _____ forces.

2. Some say that the right to _____ does not mean that everyone can carry a gun.

3. The bombing raid resulted in many _____, and many more people were still missing.

4. During the civil war, the army _____ countless atrocities.

5. After weeks of heavy fighting, a _____ was declared to allow civilians to escape.

6. The Geneva protocol bans the use of chemical _____.

7. In 1914, Germany saw Russia's mobilisation as an aggressive _____ of war.

8. Germany's _____ at Stalingrad resulted in catastrophic losses.

109

GOVERNMENT, LAW & POLITICS

hostilities Kampfhandlungen **hostile** (adj.)
When hostilities broke out in 1914, people responded with patriotic celebrations.

intelligence service Geheimdienst
British intelligence services work with the CIA.

invasion Einfall; Invasion **to invade; invader** (n.)
The 1066 Norman invasion was bloody and brutal.

massacre Massaker **to massacre**
The prime minister visited the site of a British massacre of Indians.

military Militär **military** (adj.)
The military is very interested in using robotic technology to protect soldiers' lives.

national security nationale Sicherheit
Protecting the American computer network is a national security priority.

negotiation Verhandlung **to negotiate; negotiator** (n.)
The plan is the product of months of negotiations with the White House.

to occupy s.th. etw. besetzen **occupation** (n.); **occupier** (n.)
She risked her life in occupied France during the Second World War.

prisoner of war (POW) Kriegsgefangene(r)
The last German POWs were allowed home in 1948.

soldier Soldat(in)
Over 150 Canadian soldiers have been killed in Afghanistan.

surrender Kapitulation **to surrender**
The Civil War ended with Robert E Lee's surrender on 9 April 1865.

to survive überleben **survival** (n.); **survivor** (n.)
The two soldiers somehow survived the fire.

GOVERNMENT, LAW & POLITICS

troops Truppen; Soldaten
The final US troops are to leave the country by the end of the year.

truce Waffenstillstand
The two sides have reached a truce.

warfare Kriegführung
After decades of sporadic warfare, it's time to normalize relations.

to wound s.o. jdn. verletzen   **wound** (n.); **wounded** (adj.)
The attack wounded eight soldiers.

? 54 Complete each sentence with a word from the same family as the word in brackets.

1. The two parties _____ for weeks before they came to an agreement. (negotiation)

2. British and American troops came as conquerors, but they became _____ and soon turned into protectors. (to occupy)

3. In 1940, the Belgian army _____ to the Germans. (surrender)

4. The country began to mobilise troops to protect against its _____ neighbour. (hostilities)

5. The attack left hundreds dead and thousands _____ . (to wound)

6. The Norman _____ introduced new words into the English language. (invasion)

7. A few of the villagers hid and were the only _____ of the attack. (to survive)

8. During the partition of India in 1947, thousands of people were _____ . (massacre)

111

LITERATURE • DESCRIBING LITERATURE

to address s.th. to s.o. etw. an jdn. richten
Hamlet's deeply hurtful remarks addressed to Ophelia send her into madness.

to be set in/to take place in spielen in   **setting** (n.)
Set in Mumbai, Slumdog Millionaire won eight awards at the Oscars.

classic Klassiker   **classical** (adj.)
J.D. Salinger inspired generations with his classic on teenage rebellion.

to deal with s.th./s.o. von etw./jdm. handeln
The book deals with the ethics of 'designer babies'.

eloquent wortgewandt   **eloquence** (n.)
Barack Obama is a very eloquent public speaker.

to feature zeigen; präsentieren   **feature** (n.)
Jack London's Call of the Wild features a dog as its main character.

to identify with s.o. s. mit jdm. identifizieren   **identification** (n.)
Mark Twain identified strongly with his Tom Sawyer character.

to imagine s.th.
s. etw. ausdenken/vorstellen   **imagination** (n.); **imaginative** (adj.)
Updike always returned to the imagined world of his childhood.

to undergo a change eine Veränderung durchmachen
In Dickens's A Christmas Carol, Ebenezer Scrooge undergoes a profound change.

ELEMENTS OF LITERATURE

alliteration Alliteration   **to alliterate; alliterative** (adj.)
The names of authors James Joyce and Bill Bryson are alliterations.

LITERATURE

assonance Assonanz
The assonance of "The shady lady of the night delighted in his mighty sight" is clear.

atmosphere Atmosphäre **atmospheric** (adj.)
In To Kill a Mockingbird, Lee recreates the atmosphere of the American South.

character Figur **characteristic** (n.; adj.)
Harry Rabbit Angstrom is John Updike's most famous character.

climax Höhepunkt **climactic** (adj.)
The climax of many 20th-century romance novels actually takes place in bed.

denouement Ausgang
The denouement of Treasure Island comes when the pirates find the treasure is gone.

 55 *Write the English word or expression in the space provided.*

1. wortgewandt

2. Höhepunkt

3. spielen in

4. Figur

5. Ausgang

6. von etw./jdm. handeln

7. s. etw. ausdenken/vorstellen

8. eine Veränderung durchmachen

9. etw. an jdn. richten

10. zeigen; präsentieren

LITERATURE

to describe s.th. etw. beschreiben   **description** (n.); **descriptive** (adj.)
The Red Badge of Courage describes the horrors of the American Civil War.

exposition Erläuterung
Some of Walter Scott's expositions go on for 70 pages and more.

first-person narrator Ich-Erzähler
Robinson Crusoe is a first-person narrator who can tell a good adventure story.

hero/heroine Held/Heldin   **heroism** (n.); **heroic** (adj.)
Lisbeth Salander is the heroine of the best-seller The Girl with the Dragon Tattoo.

imagery Bilder; Symbolik   **image** (n.)
Bruce Springsteen says a lot of biblical imagery enters his songs.

linguistic device Sprachmittel
A linguistic device favoured by Twain in Huckleberry Finn is the use of dialect.

narrative perspective Erzählperspektive
The author uses diaries to change the narrative perspective in the middle of the novel.

narrative technique Erzähltechnik
This book uses simplistic narrative techniques to tell a story from the perspective of a cat.

narrator Erzähler(in)   **to narrate; narration** (n.)
The story is told by three narrators.

omniscient narrator allwissende(r) Erzähler(in)
An omniscient narrator is one who knows all of the information about the story.

personification Personifikation   **to personify**
Sherlock Holmes's enemy Moriarty is often viewed as the personification of evil.

LITERATURE

plot Handlung
Shakespeare dealt with the events of his life in the plots of his plays.

point of view Erzählperspektive
The play tells the story from the point of view of the boy's smartphone.

protagonist Hauptfigur
The book's protagonist is born at the moment when India became independent.

pun Wortspiel **to pun**
Some of Shakespeare's puns don't make sense to modern audiences.

 56 *Solve the puzzle with words from these two pages.*

Across
1. A play on words
2. If the subject of many sentences in a book is "I", it has this kind of narrator.
3. The main female character in a book or play
4. The visually descriptive or figurative language that brings a work of literature to life
5. Giving human qualities to an animal or thing
6. The narrator who knows everything
7. Colloquial language and rhetorical questions are examples of linguistic _ _ _ _ _ _ _ .
8. The main events of a film, play or novel

Down
1. The leading character in a play, film or book

115

LITERATURE

resolution Auflösung · **to resolve**
After much drama, the resolution of the novel Jane Eyre is rather tame.

sequence of events Ablauf der Ereignisse
Adventure stories often begin with an unusual sequence of events.

setting Schauplatz; Kulisse · **to set (s.th. somewhere)**
An old castle at night is the perfect setting for a story as dark as Stoker's Dracula.

stylistic device Stilmittel
A stylistic device favoured by Dickens is using names that say something about a character.

subject Thema
McEwan's favourite subject is sex, yet his books are clever rather than sexy.

suspense Spannung · **suspenseful** (adj.)
A good crime novel needs a lot of suspense.

third-person narrator Er-/Sie-Erzähler
Repair manuals are written by third-person narrators – not by the dishwasher.

turning point Wendepunkt
The turning point came when she fell in love with him after years of fighting.

LITERARY FORMS

comedy Komödie · **comedian** (n.); **comic** (adj.)
The play is a comedy about young Indian office workers.

detective novel Kriminalroman
Crime writer Agatha Christie created no fewer than 66 detective novels.

drama Drama · **dramatist** (n.); **dramatic** (adj.)
George Clooney helped make ER television's most lucrative hospital drama.

fable Fabel
A traditional fable is a short story that teaches a moral lesson.

fairy tale Märchen   **fairytale** (adj.)
The Brothers Grimm wrote down many German and French fairy tales.

fictional/fictitious erfunden   **fiction** (n.) | ≠ **factual**
Rummidge is a fictional city based on Birmingham, David Lodge's workplace.

genre Gattung
The novel belongs to a new genre called 'faction': fiction based on real-life stories.

 57 *Match each word or expression with its translation.*

1. Spannung	a) resolution
2. Komödie	b) sequence of events
3. Kriminalroman	c) setting
4. Ablauf der Ereignisse	d) stylistic device
5. Märchen	e) subject
6. Gattung	f) suspense
7. Stilmittel	g) third-person narrator
8. Schauplatz; Kulisse	h) turning point
9. Fabel	i) comedy
10. Thema	j) detective novel
11. Wendepunkt	k) fable
12 Auflösung	l) fairy tale
13. erfunden	m) genre
14. Er-/Sie-Erzähler	n) fictitious/fictional

1. ____ 2. ____ 3. ____ 4. ____ 5. ____ 6. ____ 7. ____ 8. ____ 9. ____

10. ____ 11. ____ 12. ____ 13. ____ 14. ____

LITERATURE

legend Legende **legendary** (adj.)
The legend of King Arthur has delighted Britons for hundreds of years.

moving ergreifend; bewegend
To my mind, Ophelia's death is by far the most moving scene in all of Hamlet.

narrative prose Erzählprosa
The narrative prose of Truman Capote is truly powerful.

non-fiction Sachliteratur
Gaskell's biography of Charlotte Brontë belongs to the greatest works of non-fiction.

novel Roman
Thomas Keneally turned Schindler's heroic deeds into the novel Schindler's Ark.

novelist Romanschreiber
The life of Charles Dickens, Britain's greatest novelist, was recently celebrated in Portsmouth.

parable Parabel
Some of Kafka's parables are almost as short as Twitter messages.

poem Gedicht **poetry** (n.); **poet** (n.); **poetic** (adj.)
Maya Angelou's poems on race and gender were an inspiration to millions.

prose (fiction) Erzählliteratur **prosaic** (adj.)
Hardy's Under the Greenwood Tree is a classic and amusing piece of prose fiction.

sonnet Sonett
Shakespeare's sonnet no. 18 tries to make love immortal.

tragedy Tragödie **tragedian** (n.); **tragic** (adj.)
Romeo and Juliet is a classic Shakespearean tragedy.

LITERATURE

THEATRE

act Aufzug; Akt
The final act of Hamlet begins with a conversation between two gravediggers.

actor/actress Schauspieler/Schauspielerin   **acting** (n.)
Sir Anthony Hopkins is an Oscar-winning actor.

cast Besetzung   **to cast**
The novel was brought to the big screen with a cast of stars.

playwright; dramatist Dramatiker
No other playwright ever 'got under the skin of the nation' like Shakespeare.

 58 *Find the correct endings to the sentences.*

1.	A man who plays a part in a play or film is	a) the cast.
2.	If a play or film makes you sad or even makes you cry you say it is	b) a poem.
3.	A piece of literature with short lines that often rhyme is	c) moving.
4.	All the people who play parts in a play are	d) a dramatist/ playwright.
5.	A person who writes fictional books is	e) an actor.
6.	A person who writes plays is	f) a novelist.
7.	A book that tells you facts about a subject is a work of	g) prose fiction.
8.	Novels and short stories are examples of	h) non-fiction.

1. ___ 2. ___ 3. ___ 4. ___ 5. ___ 6. ___ 7. ___ 8. ___

LITERATURE

to rehearse proben **rehearsal** (n.)
The actors rehearsed the play all weekend.

scene Szene
The scene shows Jack and Rose in each other's arms at sundown.

script Drehbuch; Text (für ein Theaterstück)
Julian Fellowes often wrote food into the script of Downton Abbey.

soliloquy Monolog **to soliloquize**
Hamlet's 'To be or not to be' soliloquy is theatre's most famous monologue.

stage Bühne **to stage**
For most of the play, there were only two characters on stage.

VERSE

blank verse Blankvers
Blank verse does not rhyme, but it is often written in iambic pentameter.

iambic pentameter fünfhebiger Jambus
A new Chinese translation of Shakespeare will not be in iambic pentameter.

line Verszeile
"Shall I compare thee to a summer's day?" is one of the most famous lines in poetry.

lyrical lyrisch **lyrics** (n., pl.)
His poems have been described as works of lyrical beauty.

metre Metrum
Metre is to poetry what drummers are to rock bands.

rhyme scheme Reimschema **to rhyme**
The rhyme scheme is ABABCDCD.

LITERATURE

rhyming couplet Reimpaar
Shakespeare often ended a dramatic scene with a rhyming couplet.

rhythm Rhythmus   **rhythmic** (adj.)
The author understands the rhythms of ordinary speech.

stanza Strophe
Stanzas in poetry are like paragraphs in prose.

syllable Silbe
The first line of this poem has ten syllables.

verse form Versform
The verse forms of Asia differ radically from those used in the western world.

59 Use words and expressions from these two pages to replace the underlined words in the sentences.

1. The director still isn't satisfied with our performance, so he wants us to practise again tomorrow. _____

2. In House of Cards, the power-hungry main character reveals his thoughts in speeches to himself. _____

3. I think poetry should rhyme because it just sounds nicer; I don't like poetry that does not rhyme. _____

4. Two rhyming lines at the end of a poem give the effect of completeness.
   _____

5. Joe has been in his room all evening learning the words of the play before our first rehearsal tomorrow. _____

6. As soon as she went on to the platform for performers, she forgot that she was in a concert hall and played better than she had ever played before. _____

7. This is a very long poem with 30 groups of lines. _____

121

MEDIA · ADVERTISING

to advertise
Werbung machen   **advertising** (n.); **advertisement** (n.); **advertiser** (n.)
They usually advertise in the local newspaper.

advertising campaign Werbekampagne
Coca-Cola Christmas trucks are part of a successful advertising campaign.

to appeal to s.o. jdn. ansprechen   **appeal** (n.); **appealing** (adj.)
That kind of newspaper doesn't really appeal to me.

attention-grabbing Aufmerksamkeit erregend
The Sun almost always has an attention-grabbing headline.

brand Marke
Coca-Cola is one of the world's best-known brands.

to carry an advertisement eine Anzeige bringen
The magazine won't carry any advertisements for alcohol.

classified ad Kleinanzeige
They placed a classified ad, but no one responded.

colour supplement Farbbeilage
The Sunday paper includes a colour supplement.

deception Betrug   **to deceive; deceptive** (adj.)
This advert uses deception to sell products.

market research Marktforschung   **to research; researcher** (n.)
Their company uses market research to find out more about its customers.

to personalize/personalise (BE) **s.th.** etw. personalisieren
The Internet lets companies personalize their ads for different users.

MEDIA

to place an ad eine Anzeige schalten **placement** (n.)
The company placed ads in all of the daily newspapers.

to regulate s.th. etw. regulieren **regulation** (n.); **regulator** (n.); **regulatory** (adj.)
Adverts for alcohol and cigarettes are regulated by the government.

revenue Einnahmen
They make most of their revenue from advertisements.

60 *Complete the sentences with words and expressions from these two pages.*

1. 'Gotcha' is famous as the most _____ headline The Sun newspaper ever had.

2. If we want more sales of this product we will have to _____ it better; no one knows anything about it.

3. She was looking for a new flat, so every day, she bought a newspaper and studied the _____ .

4. There are always great photos for the recipes in the _____ _____ you get with the Sunday newspaper.

5. The journalist was guilty of _____ ; many of the people and places in his stories didn't exist.

6. People often complain about ads, but they are an important source of _____ for newspapers and magazines.

7. The Guardian newspaper has a lot of long stories, and _____ to people who are interested in politics and society.

8. Our _____ has found that the average age of our readers is 52, and that 90 per cent of them have a positive opinion of our newspaper.

NEW MEDIA

to have access to s.th. zu etw. Zugang haben **to access; accessible** (adj.)
You don't have access to that website unless you register first.

---

audio file Audiodatei
Listen to the audio file for the correct pronunciation.

---

to bookmark a website eine Webseite zu den Favoriten hinzufügen
I bookmarked all of the sites I could find on the subject.

---

to communicate with s.o. mit jdm. kommunizieren **communication** (n.)
I use Facebook to communicate with my friends.

---

connectivity Konnektivität **to connect; connection** (n.)
Have you checked your connectivity?

---

to create erstellen **creator** (n.); **creation** (n.)
I created a website to find people with the same interests.

---

to design gestalten **designer** (n.); **design** (n.)
We had our website professionally designed.

---

digital age digitales Zeitalter
Are print newspapers still relevant in a digital age?

---

digital subscription Onlineabo; Digitalabo **to subscribe**
I only have a digital subscription to the magazine.

---

to enter s.th. etw. eingeben **entry** (n.)
This website asks you to enter your personal information.

---

graphics Grafiken **graphic designer** (n.)
The graphics on that page are very simple.

---

keyword Stichwort
Enter several keywords to find information on your topic.

MEDIA

on the net/Internet im Internet
I found these pictures on the net.

online audience Onlineleserschaft   ≠ **offline audience**
She has an online audience of around 300,000 viewers.

pornography Pornografie   **pornographic** (adj.)
Many young people see pornography on the Internet.

to post s.th. online etw. ins Internet stellen   **post** (n.)
I posted this cute photo online.

? 61 *Write the English word or expression in the space provided.*

1. Audiodatei   _____

2. erstellen   _____

3. zu etw. Zugang haben   _____

4. Onlineabo   _____

5. Onlineleserschaft   _____

6. etw. eingeben   _____

7. eine Webseite zu den Favoriten hinzufügen   _____

8. im Internet   _____

9. Stichwort   _____

10. digitales Zeitalter   _____

MEDIA

privacy Datenschutz; Schutz der Privatsphäre **private** (adj.)
My online privacy is very important to me.

search engine Suchmaschine **to search**
I tried several different search engines, but I couldn't find anything.

search term Suchbegriff **to search; searcher** (n.)
Try a different search term if you're not getting enough results.

secure sicher **to secure; security** (n.) | ≠ **insecure**
We use a secure internet connection for banking.

social media soziale Medien
All the traditional media like TV channels and newspapers are now present on social media as well.

to spread verbreiten; s. ausbreiten **spread** (n.)
Stories and pictures can spread quickly on the Internet.

to surf the Internet im Internet surfen
I spent all night surfing the Internet.

unrestricted access to ungehinderter Zugang zu ≠ **restricted access**
For unrestricted access to this site, you have to register.

NEWSPAPERS & MAGAZINES

advice column Ratgeberkolumne
Many readers like to follow advice columns in their favourite newspaper.

circulation Auflage **to circulate**
The circulation of many newspapers has fallen in recent years.

column Kolumne **columnist** (n.)
Her column this week is about dogs.

MEDIA

crossword puzzle Kreuzworträtsel
They never do the crossword puzzle because it's too difficult.

editorial Leitartikel   **to edit; editor** (n.)
They didn't agree with the editorial on the war.

front page Titelseite
It was on the front page of yesterday's paper.

headline Schlagzeile   **to make headlines**
Have you seen the headlines about the election?

? 62 *Complete each sentence with a word from the same family as the word in brackets.*

1. Many people dislike online banking because they don't think it is _____ . (security)

2. The story they posted on social media _____ quickly and was seen by millions by the end of the week. (circulation)

3. Google's top _____ in 2018 was 'World Cup'. (to search)

4. I like to keep what I do on the internet _____ , so I don't use Google. (privacy)

5. Before Google, Yahoo was the most popular _____ . (to search)

6. She reads the New York Times _____ every day because it always offers an informed opinion. (editor)

7. One of the main concerns in election year was the _____ of fake news through social media. (to spread)

8. Thomas Friedman, whose articles are printed in the New York Times, is one of the world's most respected _____ . (column)

MEDIA

letter to the editor Leserbrief
He wrote a letter to the editor, but it wasn't published.

newspaper article Zeitungsartikel
She gave me an interesting newspaper article about climate change.

obituary Nachruf
My grandmother always reads the obituary page.

periodical (Fach-)Zeitschrift
I subscribe to several periodicals.

popular newspaper Massenblatt
They only read popular newspapers like The Sun and the Daily Mail.

quality newspaper seriöse Zeitung
The Guardian is one of Britain's quality newspapers.

readership Leserschaft
Our young readership enjoys articles about animals.

section Rubrik
I always look at the world news section of the paper first.

subscription fee Abogebühr **to subscribe; subscriber** (n.)
We charge a subscription fee of £45 a year.

tabloid Boulevardzeitung
Many people say that they don't like tabloids, but they read them anyway.

PUBLISHING

copyright Urheberrecht **to copyright**
All media publications are protected by copyright.

MEDIA

edition Auflage   **to edit**
The second edition of the book has some important changes and additions.

hardback/hardcover (edition) gebundene Ausgabe   ≠ **paperback**
The hardcover edition is usually a bit more expensive than the paperback.

media industry Medienbranche
Important members of the media industry will be there.

media landscape Medienlandschaft
The media landscape today is dominated by the Internet.

63 *Complete the sentences with words and expressions from these two pages.*

1. She was so angry about the article that she wrote a _____ .

2. When Pope John Paul II died, the New York Times published the longest _____ ever.

3. As a doctor, she wanted to keep up with the latest developments, so she read several _____ every month.

4. _____ newspapers like The Sun have a very large _____ .

5. Reading a _____ newspaper like The Times will keep you well informed about world events.

6. The newspaper struggled to make a profit, so they raised the _____ to $25.50 per month.

7. The _____ were full of news about the TV star's latest scandal.

8. You can't just use that photo on your website; you have to find out about the _____ first.

129

MEDIA

paperback (edition) Taschenbuch(ausgabe)
New books take a while to come out in paperback.

popular beliebt   **to popularize/popularise** (BE); **popularity** (n.)
This is one of the most popular shows on television today.

service Dienst
People are no longer interested in paying for news services.

target group Zielgruppe   **to target**
Different media have different target groups.

REPORTING

biased voreingenommen   **bias** (n.) | ≠ **unbiased**
I think the journalist is biased.

breaking news Eilmeldung
They interrupted the sitcom to report on breaking news.

to censor zensieren   **censorship** (n.); **censor** (n.)
In the US, the government cannot censor media.

to come under fire in die Kritik geraten
The paper has come under fire for its one-sided coverage.

controversial umstritten   **controversy** (n.)
Capital punishment is a very controversial issue.

to cover (über ein Thema) berichten   **coverage** (n.)
The paper didn't cover this story at all.

critic Kritiker   **criticism** (n.); **critique** (n.); **critical** (adj.)
All of the critics loved this film.

MEDIA

current affairs Tagesgeschehen
The magazine mostly covers current affairs.

editor (Chef-)Redakteur(in)   **to edit**
The editor decided not to print the article.

factual sachlich   **fact** (n.)
A newspaper mostly contains factual reporting.

freedom of the press Pressefreiheit
Freedom of the press is very important in our country.

? 64 *Use words and expressions from these two pages to replace the underlined words in the sentences.*

1. In this article, the journalist <u>reports on</u> the presidential election in the US.
   _____

2. The report was interesting but very <u>one-sided</u> because the journalist only interviewed the strikers. _____

3. The report on prisons was incomplete because the government had <u>cut out</u> the parts it didn't approve of. _____

4. The president <u>was criticised</u> for starting a trade war that hurt businesses.
   _____

5. She reads the newspaper every day, so she knows a lot about <u>events of political or social interest.</u> _____

6. The <u>reviewer</u> said the film had some good acting, but the plot was boring.
   _____

7. All the events mentioned in this film are <u>real</u>, but we have changed some of the names of people. _____

MEDIA

gossip Klatsch   **to gossip; gossip columnist** (n.); **gossipy** (adj.)
He always looks at the gossip page first.

to invade s.o.'s privacy
in jds. Privatsphäre eindringen   **invasion** (n.); **invader** (n.); **invasive** (adj.)
The journalists invaded our privacy after the arrest.

issue Ausgabe
Have you read this week's issue of Time magazine yet?

journalist Journalist(in)   **journalism** (n.)
Several journalists waited to speak with the police.

to mislead irreführen   **misleading** (adj.)
Voters were misled about the consequences of leaving the EU.

news source Nachrichtenquelle
What's your favourite news source?

objective objektiv   ≠ **subjective**
This article doesn't seem very objective.

one-sided einseitig   ≠ **unbiased**
This story is completely one-sided.

perceptive scharfsichtig   **to perceive; perception** (n.)
The reporter asked the prime minister some very perceptive questions.

to publish s.th. etw. veröffentlichen   **publisher** (n.); **publication** (n.)
They published the story even though we asked them not to.

quote/quotation Zitat   **to quote**
The article begins with a quote from Barack Obama.

to report (on) berichten (über)   **reporter** (n.); **reporting** (n.); **report** (n.)
In our 10 o'clock news programme, we report on the state visit.

MEDIA

review Rezension **to review; reviewer** (n.)
Her book sold a lot of copies but got bad reviews.

rumour (BE)/**rumor** (AE) Gerücht
This article is just a lot of rumours, there are no real facts.

satirical satirisch **to satirize/satirise** (BE); **satire** (n.); **satirist** (n.)
He writes a satirical column for a Sunday paper.

 65 *Complete the grid with words from the word families. A dash (–) means you don't have to find a word. If there are two nouns, write down both.*

noun	verb	adjective
	to gossip	
invasion		
–	to mislead	
	to publish	–
reviewer		–
	to satirise	
	to issue	–
	to quote	–
journalist	–	

MEDIA

sensationalist reißerisch **sensation** (n.); **sensational** (adj.)
Stories in tabloid newspapers are often very sensationalist.

thought-provoking zum Nachdenken anregend **to provoke; provocation** (n.)
This editorial is very thought-provoking.

TV · RADIO

BBC/British Broadcasting Corporation öffentlich-rechtliche Rundfunk- und Fernsehanstalt in Großbritannien
I get all of my news from the BBC.

to broadcast s.th. etw. senden **broadcaster** (n.); **broadcast** (n.)
They broadcast the news from their London studios.

broadcasting company Rundfunk- und Fernsehanstalt
The broadcasting company owns several television stations.

cable TV Kabelfernsehen
I usually only watch cable TV.

commercial kommerziell **commercial** (n.)
Even public media are becoming more and more commercial these days.

commercial break Werbepause
There will be no commercial breaks during the film.

commercial TV Privatfernsehen
Commercial TV is paid for by advertisements.

contestant Wettkandidat(in) **to contest; contest** (n.)
She's been a contestant on six game shows.

documentary Dokumentarfilm **to document**
They learned a lot about life in Australia from the documentary.

episode Folge
This is the funniest episode of the series I've ever seen.

mass media Massenmedien
The mass media are usually very quick to report on important events.

the news Nachrichten
I like to listen to the news in the morning.

producer Produzent   **to produce; production** (n.)
The producer has increased the budget for our show.

 66 *Solve the puzzle using words from these two pages.*

Across

1. Satellite TV is often cheaper than _ _ _ _ _ TV, but it can be affected by bad weather.
3. During the commercial _ _ _ _ _, she went into the kitchen and put the kettle on.
4. It was my favourite soap opera and I was really sad when the last _ _ _ _ _ _ _ came and it ended.
5. Designed to provoke interest and excitement, but not always truthful
6. Radio, television and newspapers are all examples of mass _ _ _ _ _.
7. A factual film about real events
8. A programme on TV or radio that tells you about the events of the day
9. A person who takes part in a games show or talent show

Down

2. The football match was _ _ _ _ _ _ _ _ live on television.

MEDIA

programme (BE)/**program** (AE) Sendung **programming** (n.)
My favourite programme comes on Tuesday nights.

public sector broadcaster öffentlich-rechtliche Rundfunk- und Fernsehanstalt
The BBC was the first public sector broadcaster in the UK.

satellite dish Satellitenschüssel
Almost every house on the street has a satellite dish on the roof.

series Serie
She's watched every episode of the series.

soap (opera) Seifenoper
We watch the soaps every afternoon.

subtitle Untertitel **to subtitle**
You can turn on the subtitles if you don't speak French.

to transmit s.th. etw. übertragen **transmission** (n.); **transmitter** (n.)
All the TV channels transmitted the royal wedding.

TV listings Fernsehprogramm
Have you seen the TV listings?

TV set Fernsehgerät
They have a large TV set in every room.

viewer Zuschauer(in) **to view**
Almost 1 million viewers watched the show last night.

67 *Use these verbs from the 'media' section of this book to complete the sentences. Make sure you use the correct forms.*

have • mislead • broadcast • publish • bookmark • search • surf • carry • create • enter • spread • personalise • post • censor

1. The news was fake, but that didn't stop it _____ very rapidly on social media.
2. They were very disappointed that they didn't _____ access to the internet in their room.
3. If you need more information on the electoral system, why don't you _____ the internet?
4. This website is really useful, and I've _____ it so I can find it quickly when I need it.
5. The politician told the truth about his income, but he _____ the public on other issues.
6. Yesterday's edition _____ a full-page advert for the new car.
7. Emma _____ a beautiful website for her translation business.
8. These photos are really good, but they are too personal to _____ online.
9. He didn't really concentrate on the TV programme because he was _____ the internet on his tablet at the same time.
10. The film about life in North Korea was heavily _____ so that none of the problems were shown.
11. The Last Night of the Proms is _____ live to viewers on every continent.
12. Please _____ your name and address in the fields below.
13. The hardcover edition was _____ last year, and the paperback will follow in June.
14. Cookies help us to _____ the ads we show you.

7 OUR WORLD · CITIES

accommodation Unterkunft   **to accommodate (s.o.)**
She has lived in rented accommodation ever since she left her parents' home.

business district Geschäftsviertel
Almost 30% of driving in business districts is spent looking for a parking spot.

commuter Pendler   **to commute; commute** (n.)
Many commuters drive to work without passing a shop.

congestion Stau   **to be congested**
Congestion has caused the average speed of trips to fall to 24.6 miles per hour.

cosmopolitan weltbürgerlich
Dallas-Fort Worth presents itself as a cosmopolitan, modern metropolis.

crowded übervölkert; überfüllt   **crowd** (n.)
He grew up playing in the crowded streets of Manhattan's Chinatown.

(municipal/city) council Stadtverwaltung **councillor** (n. BE); **councilor** (n. AE)
The city council will open a £15m museum this April.

development Bebauung   **to develop; developer** (n.)
There has been a loss of green spaces through development.

housing Wohnungen   **to house**
In some parts of the city, 80% of housing is empty.

inhabitant/resident Einwohner   **to inhabit/reside**
Nearly half of the city's residents are Asian.

living conditions Lebensbedingungen
Victoria Park became popular with working-class families taking a break from the living conditions in the East End.

luxury flat Luxuswohnung **luxury** (n.); **luxurious** (adj.)
The company is planning to build a 54-storey tower block with luxury flats.

overcrowding Überfüllung; Übervölkerung **overcrowded** (adj.)
The new homes are likely to make school overcrowding worse.

to preserve s.th. etw. erhalten **preservation** (n.)
The house has been preserved as the family kept it.

public transport (system) öffentliche Verkehrsmittel
Many people drive even when they know that public transport would be quicker.

68 Use words and expressions from these two pages to replace the underlined words in the sentences.

1. Helen's got a new job in London and now she is looking for <u>somewhere to live</u>.

2. The train strike made life very difficult for <u>people who travel to work</u>.

3. The new <u>building project</u> had housing for the wealthy and also for those on low incomes.

4. She enjoyed working in London, but she found the streets far too <u>full of people</u>.

5. Munich has very good <u>buses, trams and trains</u>.

6. The <u>people who live here</u> come from many different countries.

7. We value the historic buildings in our town and our aim is to <u>keep them in their existing state</u> for future generations.

8. They were very late because of the <u>queue of cars</u> on the motorway.

OUR WORLD

residential area Wohnviertel **resident** (n.); **residence** (n.)
The government is trying to keep the birds away from residential areas.

rural ländlich ≠ **urban**
About 65% of Africa's people live in rural areas.

rush hour Stoßzeit
There is a rush hour of bicycles in the morning.

to surround s.th. etw. umgeben **surrounding** (adj.)
The town is cut in two by train lines and surrounded by hills.

tower block Hochhaus
Many famous New Yorkers live in the trendy tower blocks of Chelsea and SoHo.

underground (BE)/**subway** (AE) U-Bahn
About 18 per cent of London workers travel on the London Underground.

urban growth Städtewachstum
Urban growth rates are highest in the developing world.

urbanization/urbanisation (BE) Verstädterung
Some economists say that India needs urbanization if it is ever to become a great economic power.

ENVIRONMENT

adverse effect negative Wirkung
Emissions cuts could stop the adverse effects of climate change.

to avert s.th. etw. verhindern **aversion** (n.)
Billions of trees need to be planted to avert climate change.

biodegradable biologisch abbaubar
Biodegradable waste gets broken down naturally.

on the brink of extinction vom Aussterben bedroht   **extinct** (adj.)
Black rhinos are on the brink of extinction.

carbon dioxide (CO_2) Kohlendioxid
Every flip of a light switch adds carbon dioxide to the air.

CFCs/chlorofluorocarbons FCKW
Scientists asked how the ozone layer might be affected by CFCs.

climate change Klimawandel
Climate change is likely to make extreme weather events more common.

69 *Write the English word or expression in the space provided.*

1. etw. umgeben

2. Hochhaus

3. biologisch abbaubar

4. Verstädterung

5. Stoßzeit

6. negative Wirkung

7. ländlich

8. vom Aussterben bedroht

9. etw. verhindern

10. Wohnviertel

conservation Erhaltung; Schutz   **to conserve**
The new conservation strategy should try to recreate the traditional territory of the bison.

to consume s.th. etw. verbrauchen   **consumer** (n.); **consumption** (n.)
The power plants would consume 1.3 billion gallons of water a year.

to contaminate s.th. etw. verseuchen   **contamination** (n.)
Radioactive materials contaminated the food and water supply.

to contribute to s.th. zu etw. beitragen   **contribution** (n.); **contributor** (n.)
Some studies say that global warming contributes to extreme weather.

deforestation Entwaldung
Environmentalists are worried that the new law will speed up deforestation.

destruction Zerstörung   **to destroy; to destruct; destructive** (adj.)
Politicians promised to stop the destruction of rainforests by 2030.

detergent Waschmittel
Workers began to clean the birds using hot water and a mild dish detergent.

devastating effect verheerende Auswirkung   **to devastate; devastation** (n.)
The accident is also likely to have a devastating effect in Japan.

disaster Katastrophe   **disastrous** (adj.)
Warnings of safety at the factory were ignored for years before the disaster.

disease Krankheit   **diseased** (adj.)
Healthy pigs are given low levels of antibiotics to prevent disease.

to dispose of s.th. etw. entsorgen   **disposal** (n.); **disposable** (adj.)
It could take at least eight years to dispose of waste that has been there since the 1980s.

drought Dürre
During drought years in the United States, less water will be sent to Mexico.

emissions Schadstoffausstoß
Coal-fired power plants are the nation's largest source of greenhouse gas emissions.

to emit ausstoßen   **emission** (n.)
The new engines emit less carbon dioxide than older models.

endangered species vom Aussterben bedrohte Arten
Last year, the birds were officially taken off the endangered species list.

70 Complete each sentence with a word from the same family as the word in brackets.

1. The _____ of meat will probably increase in Asia as people become wealthier. (to consume)

2. Methane from the stomachs of cattle makes a big _____ to global warming. (to contribute)

3. Environmental organisations called for a halt to the _____ of the rain forest. (to destroy)

4. Burning coal has _____ consequences for the air we breathe. (disaster)

5. The city wanted to improve its waste _____ system so that more rubbish could be recycled. (to dispose)

6. Carbon dioxide _____ are a major cause of global warming. (to emit)

7. The aim of the national park is to _____ the unique habitats and endangered species. (conservation)

8. The _____ caused by the drought could be seen everywhere – in dried-up rivers and dead plants and animals. (devastating)

143

energy-efficient energiesparend **energy-efficiency** (n.)
Many producers of energy-efficient lighting have already moved to China.

environment Umwelt **environmentalist** (n.); **environmental** (adj.)
Paul McCartney says that just one meat-free day per week could improve the environment.

environmentally friendly umweltfreundlich
Many men are turning to a healthier and more environmentally friendly mode of transport.

to exceed s.th. etw. übersteigen **excess** (n.); **excessive** (adj.)
Levels of air pollution in Delhi have exceeded those in Beijing.

exhaust fumes Auspuffgase
Exhaust fumes from cars are the biggest single contributor to rising pollution levels in Delhi.

fertilizer/fertiliser (BE) Dünger **to fertilize/fertilise** (BE)
New equipment can put fertilizer in the ground during planting.

flooding Überschwemmung(en) **to flood; flood** (n.)
The powerful storm caused flooding.

food chain Nahrungskette
After being eaten by fish, the pollutants enter the food chain.

fossil fuel fossiler Brennstoff **to fossilize/fossilise** (BE)
Governments have not found enough good alternatives to fossil fuels.

fuel Treib-/Brennstoff **to fuel**
Many people like the idea of burning waste to create fuel.

glacier Gletscher **glacial** (adj.)
The glaciers that feed the rivers are melting.

groundwater Grundwasser
Pollution of the groundwater with chemicals can cause diseases.

habitat Lebensraum
These new habitats are expected to provide homes for birds.

harmful schädlich   **to harm; harm** (n.)
The filter kills 99.9% of harmful bacteria.

heatwave Hitzewelle
The heatwave of 2003 is likely to become the norm by the end of the century.

 71 *Match each word or expression with its translation.*

1. umweltfreundlich
2. Auspuffgase
3. Überschwemmung(en)
4. Hitzewelle
5. Grundwasser
6. Umwelt
7. schädlich
8. Gletscher
9. Dünger
10. Treib-/Brennstoff
11. Lebensraum
12. fossiler Brennstoff
13. energiesparend
14. Nahrungskette
15. etw. übersteigen

a) energy-efficient
b) environment
c) to exceed s.th.
d) environmentally friendly
e) exhaust fumes
f) fertilizer/fertiliser
g) flooding
h) food chain
i) fossil fuel
j) heatwave
k) glacier
l) groundwater
m) habitat
n) harmful
o) fuel

1. ____ 2. ____ 3. ____ 4. ____ 5. ____ 6. ____ 7. ____ 8. ____ 9. ____

10. ____ 11. ____ 12. ____ 13. ____ 14. ____ 15. ____

OUR WORLD

hurricane Wirbelsturm
New Orleans is still living with the effects of Hurricane Katrina.

ice sheet Eisschild
It would take more than 1,000 years to melt the ice sheet in west Antarctica.

impact Auswirkung — **to impact**
The park management plan also points out the environmental impact of climbers.

incinerator (Müll-)Verbrennungsanlage — **to incinerate**
Norwegians are accepting rubbish from other countries to feed their incinerators.

irreversible unumkehrbar — ≠ **reversible**
Will humans cause irreversible environmental damage?

landfill Mülldeponie
About half of UK waste ends up in landfill.

litter Müll — **to litter; litterbug** (n.)
More than 2 million pieces of litter are dropped in Britain every day.

logging Holzwirtschaft — **logger** (n.)
The country has slowed deforestation by fighting illegal logging.

natural resources natürliche Ressourcen; Bodenschätze
Alaska is economically dependent on its natural resources.

nuclear power Atomkraft
Six years after Fukushima, Japan has turned away from nuclear power.

oil spill Ölteppich — **to spill**
It could take years to clean up the oil spill in the Gulf of Mexico.

organic farming ökologischer Anbau
Organic farming does not always mean more environmentally friendly farming.

OUR WORLD

ozone layer Ozonschicht
There are signs that the ozone layer is beginning to recover.

packaging Verpackung **to package; package** (n.)
Only 30 per cent of plastic packaging is recycled.

pesticide Schädlingsbekämpfungsmittel **pest** (n.)
Bumblebees have declined due to the use of pesticides.

72 *Put the letters in brackets in the correct order to find the word that completes the sentence.*

1. The weather forecast warned that a _____ was approaching the coast of Florida. **(cuaihrren)**

2. I don't like using chemicals in the garden, but we need this _____ to get rid of the caterpillars. **(edtecipsi)**

3. If we recycle more of our rubbish, less of it will go to _____ . **(lnllfadi)**

4. These biscuits have so much _____ : there's a box and each one is wrapped in plastic. **(iakpgacgn)**

5. The damage already done to the rain forest is _____ , so we have to protect what is left. **(bsrrvreielei)**

6. The rubbish that isn't recycled is taken to the _____ and burned. **(otnnireicar)**

7. _____ farming produces healthier food, but it's much more expensive too. **(ragionc)**

to poison s.o./s.th. jdn./etw. vergiften   **poison** (n.); **poisonous** (adj.)
Young workers were poisoned by the chemical.

pollutant Schadstoff
No other pollutant ruins nearly as many lives in industrialised countries as noise.

to pollute s.th. etw. verschmutzen
The last thing our polluted oceans need is a new industry destroying the seabed.

pollution Umweltverschmutzung
More cycle paths will mean less traffic, less pollution and more seats on the Tube.

power station/plant Kraftwerk
At least four new power stations are being planned around the UK to burn vegetable oils.

precipitation Niederschlag
Extremes of precipitation have increased as the planet warms and more water evaporates from the oceans.

to protect schützen   **protection** (n.); **protective** (adj.)
People need to protect themselves from the sun.

ray Strahl
The Earth's ozone layer protects all life from the damaging effects of ultraviolet rays.

to recover s.th. etw. zurückgewinnen   **recovery** (n.)
Plastic rubbish made up about 60 per cent of the waste recovered.

to recycle s.th. etw. wiederverwerten   **recyclable** (adj.)
Paper and cardboard, food, garden waste and plastics have to be recycled.

renewable erneuerbar   **to renew**
Google has spent hundreds of millions of dollars on renewable energy such as solar power.

to be at risk of extinction vom Aussterben bedroht sein   **extinct** (adj.)
Koalas are at risk of extinction due to climate change and human development.

sea level Meeresspiegel
Some of Australia's beaches are in danger of being lost due to rising sea levels.

sewage treatment plant Kläranlage   **sewage** (n.)
Waste goes through sewage treatment plants.

skin cancer Hautkrebs
Extreme sunbathing has led to an increase in skin cancer.

73 *Which words or expressions from these two pages mean ...?*

1. To use something like glass or plastic again

2. Rain, snow and sleet

3. Adjective for energy sources like wind and sun

4. To be in danger of dying out

5. A place where waste water is treated

6. A substance that can make you ill or kill you

7. To contaminate air or water with harmful substances

8. A very serious skin disease

9. An installation that produces electricity

10. A line of light or heat coming from a bright source

OUR WORLD

soil Erde; Boden **to soil; soiled** (adj.)
The potatoes get their special flavour from the island's soil.

soil erosion Bodenerosion **to erode**
Visitors to spots such as the Cliffs of Moher in Ireland can cause soil erosion.

to sort rubbish Müll trennen
Rubbish imported from the UK and Ireland may not be so carefully sorted.

species Spezies; Art
The region is home to thousands of plant species found nowhere else in the world.

stock Bestand
Overfishing is reducing local stocks of anchovies.

surface Oberfläche
Tropical forests cover 15 per cent of the world's land surface.

sustainable nachhaltig **to sustain; sustainability** (n.)
The company plans to introduce sustainable fish products.

target Ziel **to target**
Countries have agreed on a target to limit the damage from global warming.

toxic giftig **toxicity** (n.); **toxin** (n.)
Electronics companies use toxic chemicals in smartphones, televisions, tablets, computers and cables.

to waste s.th. etw. verschwenden **waste** (n.); **wasteful** (adj.)
Leaving a machine on when you're not using it wastes electricity.

water supply Wasserversorgung **to supply**
The South of England has real problems with water supply.

wildfire Flächenbrand
The wildfires have forced thousands from their homes.

OUR WORLD

GEOGRAPHY

above/below sea level über/unter dem Meeresspiegel
None of the islands lie more than two meters above sea level.

arid trocken
Water is valuable in arid areas.

to border (on) grenzen an **border** (n.)
A total of 34 animals have been killed in the area bordering the park.

? 74 Use words and expressions from these two pages to replace the underlined words in the sentences.

1. Death Valley is not only very hot, it's also extremely <u>dry</u>. _____

2. This <u>earth</u> is very good for growing cabbages. _____

3. The new houses used recycled materials and little energy, so they were <u>not using up too many natural resources</u>. _____

4. Yellowstone Park is a rich habitat with many <u>kinds</u> of animals and plants. _____

5. We don't just throw everything in the dustbin, we <u>separate plastic, paper and waste</u> first. _____

6. The power company's <u>goal</u> was to produce 50 per cent of energy from renewable sources. _____

7. The <u>poisonous</u> fumes were a danger to the health of residents in the nearby town. _____

OUR WORLD

border/frontier Grenze
China is improving the infrastructure around its frontiers.

the British Isles die Britischen Inseln
The town is one of the only places in the British Isles where you can see killer whales from the shore.

canyon Schlucht
The Grand Canyon is one of the natural wonders of the world.

cliff Klippe; Felsen
Thousands of seabirds sit on the island's cliffs.

countryside ländliche Gegend; das Land
Millions of people are moving from the countryside to cities.

county Grafschaft (BE); Landkreis (AE)
Road signs in the county are in Cornish and English.

to cover an area s. über ein Gebiet erstrecken
The park covers an area of more than 3.6 million hectares.

desert Wüste **desertification** (n.)
Most of Qatar's land is desert.

district Gebiet
The district receives water from the river for its farmers.

the English Channel der Ärmelkanal
The English Channel is an area of sea between England and France.

fertile fruchtbar **to fertilize/fertilise** (BE); **fertility** (n.) | ≠ **infertile**
The communities are fighting over one of the last pieces of fertile land.

highlands Hochland ≠ **lowlands**
The couple live in the Highlands, with woodland and waterfalls on their land.

in the north/south im Norden/Süden
Millions of African Americans moved to cities in the north during the 20th century.

inland im Inland; Binnen- **inland** (n.)
The fish swim up rivers to reach the inland waterways.

lush üppig
With its white beaches, lush plants and clear waters, the island seems like paradise.

75 *Complete the sentences with words and expressions from these two pages.*

1. After crossing the _____ from France, the first thing they saw were the white _____ of Dover.

2. The land was very _____ and the villagers were able to grow all the vegetables they needed.

3. Camels are well adapted to the _____ because they don't need much water.

4. Cornwall has pretty towns and villages and above all, beautiful _____ _____ with rolling hills and green fields.

5. The British Isles _____ of more than 315,000 km².

6. In the rainy south, the country has _____ green forests filled with exotic plants and birds.

7. Surrey is Britain's wealthiest _____, profiting from being near London.

8. We spent the first three days in Edinburgh but then we drove north to the Scottish _____.

OUR WORLD

marshy sumpfig **marsh** (n.)
British colonists landed on a marshy island in Virginia in 1607.

mountain range Gebirgskette **mountaineer** (n.)
Marco Polo's journey across mountain ranges opened the eyes of Europe to the wonders of China.

mountainous bergig
The Pennine Way follows the mountainous 'backbone of England'.

natural disaster Naturkatastrophe
Hurricane Katrina created the worst natural disaster in American history.

north/south of nördlich/südlich von
The city is 65 miles north of Dublin.

on/off the coast an/vor der Küste **coastal** (adj.)
The penguins live on the coast of Argentina.

plain Ebene
The wild horses on the American plain are living symbols of the spirit of the West.

plateau Hochebene
The high plateau of southern Colorado is one of the sunniest spots in the nation.

prairie Prärie; Grasebene
Intensively farmed prairies have been very bad for nature.

to be situated/located s. befinden **location** (n.)
The island is situated close to the coast.

slope Hang **to slope**
Snow remains on the northern slopes.

swamp Sumpf · **swampy** (adj.)
The animals live in the swamps of the Amazon river.

temperate gemäßigt
Los Angeles, California, has a very temperate climate.

wilderness Wildnis
The wilderness is being destroyed by new roads.

? 76 *Find words and expressions on these two pages that match the definitions.*

1. Something very bad that happens, like an earthquake or a hurricane

2. Adjective that describes a climate that is neither very hot nor very cold

3. Large area of grassland, especially in North America

4. An area where there are no buildings, farms or people

5. The land that is next to the sea

6. Adjective that describes a country or region with lots of mountains

7. Adjective that describes an area of low-lying land that is often wet

8. A large area of flat land with few trees

8 SCIENCE, HEALTH & TECHNOLOGY
BIOTECHNOLOGY • GENETICS

to **breed** s.th. etw. züchten   **breed** (n.)
One of the goals of genetic research is to breed human stem cells.

to **conduct** durchführen   **conductor** (n.)
Researchers argue that it's necessary to conduct animal experiments.

controversial issue strittiges Thema   **controversy** (n.)
Genetic research has always been a controversial issue.

crop Feldfrucht; Ernte(ertrag)
Improving crops is one of the main goals of biotechnology.

to **cross species** Arten kreuzen
Different species of plants are sometimes crossed to create new ones.

to **cure** s.o. of a disease jdn. von einer Krankheit heilen   **cure** (n.)
Genetics may help cure people of diseases in the future.

to **decode** s.th. etw. entschlüsseln
It has taken science a long time to decode the human genome.

defective gene fehlerhaftes Gen   **defect** (n.)
Some parents want to know if their child has a defective gene before its birth.

to **determine** s.th. etw. bestimmen   **determination** (n.); **determiner** (n.)
Gene decoding is used to determine the genetic make-up of living beings.

disease Krankheit   **diseased** (adj.)
Some diseases are genetic: children are born with them in their genes.

gene Gen   **genetics** (n.); **genetic** (adj.)
A gene is a part of one's DNA.

SCIENCE, HEALTH & TECHNOLOGY

genetic disorder genetische Störung
Trisomy-21, or Down's syndrome, is a genetic disorder.

genetic test Gentest
A genetic test identifies changes in chromosomes, genes, or proteins.

GM (genetically modified) gentechnisch verändert
Genetically modified organisms get few diseases and grow very quickly.

to heal s.o./s.th. jdn. heilen
In earlier times, plants and herbs were used to heal people.

 77 *Circle the best of the two underlined words to complete the sentences.*

1. The scientists did / conducted an experiment to measure the growth of bacteria.

2. We guarantee that none of our animals are fed with genetically modified / changed crops.

3. Science has helped the world to produce better plants / crops to feed the world.

4. Thanks to modern medicines, he was healed / cured of a disease that would have been fatal decades ago.

5. The baby had a lot of health problems due to a defective / faulty gene.

6. Thanks to ultrasound, it is now often possible to decide / determine a baby's sex before it is born.

7. It took thousands of scientists 10 years and $3bn to decode / solve the first human genome.

8. Most genetic sicknesses / disorders are the result of a mutation in one gene.

SCIENCE, HEALTH & TECHNOLOGY

herbicide resistant resistent gegen Unkrautvernichtungsmittel
Genetically modified plants are generally more herbicide resistant.

human reproductive cloning reproduktives Klonen von Menschen
Human reproductive cloning still raises many difficult ethical questions.

to implant s.th. into s.th. etw. in etw. implantieren   **implant** (n.)
Recently, scientists successfully implanted human cells into a pig's embryo.

in vitro fertilisation (IVF) künstliche Befruchtung
In vitro fertilisation can help people who normally would not be able to have children.

infertile unfruchtbar   **infertility** (n.) | ≠ **fertile**
Both women's eggs and men's sperm can be infertile, making it very difficult for some couples to have children.

to inherit s.th. from s.o. etw. von jdm. erben   **inheritance** (n.)
I inherited blue eyes and dark hair from my father.

insemination Befruchtung   **to inseminate**
Eggs and sperm have to be kept at the right temperature until insemination.

lab(oratory) Labor
One day it could be possible to grow entire human organs in labs.

long-/short-term effect langfristige/kurzfristige Auswirkung
The long-term effects of genetic manipulation are often unclear.

malformation Missbildung   **to be malformed**
Malformation in foetuses can be detected very early on today.

mammal Säugetier
Dolly the sheep was the first mammal ever to be successfully cloned.

SCIENCE, HEALTH & TECHNOLOGY

to modify s.th. genetically etw. genetisch verändern **modification** (n.)
Boyer and Cohen were the first to genetically modify an organism, in 1973.

mutation Mutation; genetische Veränderung **to mutate**
Genetic modification brings the risk of unwanted mutation.

organ donor Organspender(in) **to donate; donation** (n.)
It can be very difficult and take a very long time to find a suitable organ donor.

pest Schädling
Pests are one of the reasons for genetically modifying plants.

78 Write the English word or expression in the space provided.

1. unfruchtbar

2. langfristige/kurzfristige Auswirkung

3. Missbildung

4. Labor

5. Säugetier

6. Organspender(in)

7. resistent gegen Unkraut-vernichtungsmittel

8. Schädling

9. Befruchtung

10. etw. von jdm. erben

SCIENCE, HEALTH & TECHNOLOGY

to raise a moral concern eine moralische Frage aufwerfen **morality** (n.)
Cloning raises a lot of moral concerns for many people.

to reject s.th. etw. abstoßen **rejection** (n.)
Human bodies sometimes reject transplanted organs.

reproduction Fortpflanzung **to reproduce; reproductive** (adj.)
Biotechnologies and what they mean for human reproduction raise legal, ethical and social questions.

resistance to s.th. Widerstandsfähigkeit/Resistenz gegen etw. **to be resistant**
Genetically modified plants have a much higher resistance to pests and diseases.

to screen s.o. for a disease jdn. auf eine Krankheit untersuchen **screening** (n.)
Blood tests can screen babies for many diseases at birth.

stem cell research Stammzellenforschung **to research**
Stem cell research is especially important in the field of cancer treatment.

to stem from s.th. von etw. stammen
It is widely believed that humans stem from apes.

surrogate mother Leihmutter
Women who cannot have children themselves sometimes use a surrogate mother.

technique Methode; Verfahren
Using stem cells to fight cancer is a relatively new technique.

tissue Gewebe
Damaged skin and muscles can now be repaired using tissue grown in a lab.

transplant Transplantation **to transplant; transplantation** (n.)
The first successful live organ transplant was achieved in 1954.

vaccine Impfstoff **to vaccinate; vaccination** (n.)
Genetic research can help with developing more effective vaccines.

SCIENCE, HEALTH & TECHNOLOGY

weed Unkraut   **to weed**
One effect of genetically modifying plants is that weeds can also become stronger.

yield Ertrag   **to yield**
Genetically modified organisms typically bring higher yields than regular crops.

HEALTH

(doctor's) appointment (Arzt-)Termin
I'll be late tomorrow because I have a doctor's appointment at 9 o'clock.

79 Use the verbs below – they are all on these two pages – to complete the sentences. Make sure you use the correct forms.

stem • reject • research • screen • vaccinate • raise • yield • transplant

1. The company is _____ new ways of treating cancer.
2. Plants that have been genetically modified often _____ bigger crops.
3. Modern breeds of dogs, everything from a Dalmation to a dachshund, _____ from wolves.
4. The use of surrogate mothers as a solution to childlessness _____ moral concerns.
5. In the UK, women over 50 are _____ for breast cancer every three years.
6. More organs could be _____ and more lives saved if we had more donors.
7. Transplant patients have to take drugs that stop their bodies _____ the new organ.
8. Parents were told that their children should be _____ against measles to protect other children as well as their own child.

SCIENCE, HEALTH & TECHNOLOGY

abortion Abtreibung **to abort**
Some religious and conservative groups are against abortion.

to ache schmerzen **ache** (n.)
My back has been aching for days now. I should really see a doctor.

addict (Drogen-)Süchtige/r **to become addicted; addiction** (n.); **addictive** (adj.)
Drug addicts often become homeless.

to age altern **ageing** (BE)/**aging** (AE)
Most people want to age in a healthy way.

allergy Allergie **allergic** (adj.)
I'm sorry, I can't eat these cookies: I have a nut allergy.

anorexia Magersucht **anorexic** (adj.)
Many girls in their teens suffer from anorexia because of psychological problems.

approach Methode; Herangehensweise **to approach**
My approach to staying healthy is a balanced diet and daily exercise.

to be at risk of doing s.th. Gefahr laufen, etw. zu tun **to risk (s.th.); risky** (adj.)
Many people over 60 are at risk of having a heart attack.

balanced diet ausgewogene Ernährung **to go on a diet**
Having a balanced diet means eating different kinds of food.

beneficial vorteilhaft; förderlich **to benefit; benefit** (n.) | ≠ **bad; harmful**
Eating lots of vegetables can be very beneficial to your health.

birth Geburt **to give birth**
Chicago hospitals have noticed an increase in births.

birth control/contraception (Empfängnis-)Verhütung **contraceptive** (n.; adj.)
Female sterilisation is the most common form of birth control in India.

SCIENCE, HEALTH & TECHNOLOGY

birth rate Geburtenrate
The long, cold winter of 2009/2010 was followed by a very high birth rate the following autumn.

bulimia Bulimie **bulimic** (n.; adj.)
I suffered from bulimia from the age of 17 and lost a lot of weight.

to be a burden on society der Gesellschaft zur Last fallen **to burden** (s.o.)
Today the elderly are often seen as a burden on society.

80 *Complete each sentence with a word from the same family as the word in brackets.*

1. Heroin is a dangerous drug because it is highly _____. (addict)

2. Hannah had to be very careful about eating out because she was _____ to peanuts. (allergy)

3. A balanced diet and plenty of exercise is a good way to _____ a healthier lifestyle. (approach)

4. James was very ill and needed a lot of help; he hoped that he wouldn't _____ his family with too much responsibility for him. (burden)

5. _____ is key to reducing the unsustainable birth rate and the resulting negative impacts on the economy. (contraceptive)

6. Girls who suffer from eating disorders like anorexia and bulimia are at _____ of long-term health problems. (to risk)

7. His tooth had had a hole for some weeks, and now it began to _____ badly. (ache)

8. This cream promises to reduce wrinkles and other signs of _____ and has great _____ for your skin. (to age; beneficial)

SCIENCE, HEALTH & TECHNOLOGY

to catch (a) cold s. erkälten
You don't look too good: have you caught a cold?

condition Leiden
I have a heart condition, so I have to be careful about what kind of exercise I do.

contagious ansteckend
Viral infections are often extremely contagious.

cough Husten **to cough**
Will this cough ever go away? My throat hurts already!

deadly tödlich ≈ **fatal; lethal**
In the Middle Ages, a simple cold could be deadly for people.

to decline zurückgehen **decline** (n.) | ≠ **to increase; to rise**
Deaths caused by HIV and AIDS are declining because of advanced medication.

diet Ernährung
Many people are changing their diets and eating more fruit and vegetables.

dignity Würde **dignified** (adj.)
We need to make sure that elderly people have dignity in hospital.

eating disorder Essstörung
Most eating disorders have psychological causes.

the elderly ältere Menschen **elderly** (adj.)
My grandmother has been living in a home for the elderly for five years now.

epidemic Epidemie
Aids first became an epidemic in the 1980s.

eradication Ausrottung **to eradicate**
Scientists and doctors are successfully working on the eradication of HIV/Aids.

SCIENCE, HEALTH & TECHNOLOGY

to exercise s. bewegen; Sport treiben   **exercise** (n.)
He thought that using a car to travel somewhere to exercise was absurd.

to feel under the weather s. angeschlagen fühlen
I'm leaving early today because I feel a little bit under the weather.

foetus (BE)/**fetus** (AE) Fötus   **foetal** (BE); **fetal** (AE)
Modern medicine is able to see if a child is healthy when it is still a foetus.

? 81 *Use the parts of words below to make words that replace the question marks.*

dig • con • cation • con • cline • dis • elder • de • nity • ious • order • dition • tag • ly • eradi

1. Jane had got very thin and we thought she might have an eating ? .

2. The number of mothers who die in childbirth will ? if we improve health care.

3. At the hospice, patients are able to die peacefully and in ? .

4. Please keep your children at home if they have a ? illness like measles.

5. People are living longer, and we need to help the ? live fulfilled lives.

6. Vaccination made the ? of diseases like smallpox possible.

7. George wasn't able to fly. It was too dangerous because of his heart ? .

Use the letters in the blue squares to find a doctor who performs operations.

___ ___ ___ ___ ___ ___ ___

SCIENCE, HEALTH & TECHNOLOGY

flu/influenza Grippe
I couldn't go to school this week because I had the flu.

to go/come down with s.th. an etw. erkranken
Michael came down with the flu at the weekend.

health care Gesundheitsversorgung
One of President Obama's goals was universal health care for everyone in the US.

hereditary illness Erbkrankheit
Diabetes can be a hereditary illness; if one of your parents had it, you might have it as well.

immune system Immunsystem   **immunity** (n.)
Having a good immune system helps you stay healthy.

to infect s.o. jdn. infizieren   **infection** (n.)
During flu season a simple door handle can infect a large group of people if they do not wash their hands properly.

infectious disease ansteckende Krankheit
The state offers free treatment for infectious diseases.

life expectancy Lebenserwartung
Life expectancy in wealthy countries is usually higher than in poorer countries.

loneliness Einsamkeit   **lonely** (adj.)
Many old people suffer from loneliness.

longevity Lebensdauer; Langlebigkeit
All organisms have a limited longevity.

long-term care Langzeitpflege
Elderly people with illnesses or disabilities often require long-term care.

SCIENCE, HEALTH & TECHNOLOGY

long-term care insurance Pflegeversicherung
Many people don't get long-term care insurance because they don't want to think about getting old.

malnutrition Unterernährung   **malnourishment** (n.); **malnourished** (adj.)
In poor countries, many people, especially children, suffer from malnutrition.

measles Masern
Measles is one of the leading causes of death among young children.

medicine Medizin; Medikament   **medicinal** (adj.)
Some people don't trust traditional medicine.

 82 *Find the correct endings to the sentences.*

1. People who don't get enough of the right kind of food suffer from
2. If an illness is passed from parents to children, it is
3. If people can go to the doctor without worrying about the cost, their country has a good system of
4. One childhood disease that can be prevented by vaccination is
5. A disease that is passed from person to person is
6. If you have a high temperature, aching limbs and head, and a cough you might have the
7. Some people stay healthy when everyone else is sick because they have strong
8. People who live far away from friends and family often suffer from
9. It costs a lot of money to look after older people, so the government introduced
10. People are healthier, so there has been a rise in

a) health care.
b) malnutrition.
c) hereditary.
d) flu.
e) loneliness.
f) immune systems.
g) measles.
h) life expectancy.
i) infectious.
j) long-term care insurance.

1. ___ 2. ___ 3. ___ 4. ___ 5. ___ 6. ___
7. ___ 8. ___ 9. ___ 10. ___

167

SCIENCE, HEALTH & TECHNOLOGY

mortality Sterblichkeit   **mortal** (n.); **mortal** (adj.)
The child mortality rate has sunk dramatically since the start of the 20th century.

nausea Übelkeit   **nauseated** (adj.); **nauseating** (adj.)
I knew I had the flu when the nausea started.

to neglect s.o. jdn. vernachlässigen   **neglect** (n.)
Some families neglect their elderly parents.

obesity Fettleibigkeit   **obese** (adj.)
People whose friends gain weight are at greater risk of obesity.

to overdo s.th. etw. übertreiben
It can be harmful for the body to overdo physical exercise.

pregnancy Schwangerschaft   **pregnant** (adj.)
She is seven months into her pregnancy.

to prescribe s.th. etw. verschreiben   **prescription** (n.)
The doctor prescribed me some pills for my headache.

residential care Pflegeheim
Deciding to put a relative into residential care can be a difficult step.

runny nose laufende Nase
A runny nose can be very annoying, especially when you don't have tissues.

screening Vorsorgeuntersuchung(en)   **to screen s.o. for s.th.**
People with a high genetic risk of cancer should have earlier screening.

side effect Nebenwirkung
Internet diagnoses and self-medicating can come with dangerous side effects.

slight/elevated temperature erhöhte Temperatur
You have a slight temperature, but nothing to worry about.

SCIENCE, HEALTH & TECHNOLOGY

to sneeze niesen   **sneeze** (n.)
It really must be winter, everybody is sneezing.

sore throat Halsweh
I can't say if my sore throat is from the cold air or from singing along at the concert.

to suffer from s.th. an etw. leiden   **sufferer** (n.); **suffering** (n.)
He has been suffering from back pain for years.

? 83 *Which words or expressions from these two pages mean …?*

1. The state of expecting a baby   _____

2. The state of being too fat   _____

3. A feeling of sickness   _____

4. To write down a medicine for a patient to take   _____

5. A place where old people are cared for   _____

6. To fail to care for s.o. properly   _____

7. To do too much of s.th. so that you become ill   _____

8. A mild fever   _____

9. A symptom of a cold that means you
   need a handkerchief   _____

10. Testing a group of people for a disease   _____

169

SCIENCE, HEALTH & TECHNOLOGY

treatment Behandlung **to treat**
People are often sceptical about new treatment methods.

virus Virus **viral** (adj.)
Mosquitoes can carry some viruses.

to vomit s. übergeben **vomit** (n.)
I had stomach flu last week: I vomited all day.

INFORMATION TECHNOLOGY

to attack s.o./s.th. jdn./etw. angreifen **attack** (n.); **attacker** (n.)
Cyberbullies attack people verbally in social networks.

to authenticate authentifizieren **authentication** (n.); **authentic** (adj.)
Users need to authenticate themselves to confirm their identity.

to be online 24/7 rund um die Uhr online sein
Many people today are online 24/7 because they are afraid of missing something.

to buy a licence (BE)/**license** (AE) eine Lizenz kaufen **to license**
You can buy licenses for software like Office or Photoshop online.

calculation Berechnung **to calculate**
The task involves complex calculations of the speed of the rocket.

to crash abstürzen **crash** (n.)
My computer has already crashed twice this week.

data theft Datenraub **thief** (n.)
Many people are afraid of data theft, especially when shopping and banking online.

database Datenbank
The software sucks information from databases and publishes it on Wikipedia.

SCIENCE, HEALTH & TECHNOLOGY

to design s.th. etw. entwerfen/konzipieren   **designer** (n.); **design** (n.)
In the future, parents may leave their children with robots designed to look after them.

device Gerät
If you want to use an app, you need to check if it is available for your device.

to download s.th. onto s.th. etw. auf etw. herunterladen   **download** (n.)
You can download these photos from my computer onto your smartphone.

feature Eigenschaft; Funktion   **to feature**
Most smartphones have very similar features.

 84 *Match each word or expression with its translation.*

1. authentifizieren
2. s. übergeben
3. abstürzen
4. Eigenschaft; Funktion
5. eine Lizenz kaufen
6. Virus
7. etw. entwerfen/konzipieren
8. Datenbank
9. etw. auf etw. herunterladen
10. Gerät
11. jdn./etw. angreifen
12. Behandlung
13. Datenraub
14. Berechnung
15. rund um die Uhr online sein

a) treatment
b) virus
c) to vomit
d) to attack s.o./s.th.
e) to authenticate
f) to be online 24/7
g) to buy a licence/license
h) calculation
i) to crash
j) data theft
k) to design s.th.
l) device
m) to download s.th. onto s.th.
n) feature
o) database

1. ___ 2. ___ 3. ___ 4. ___ 5. ___ 6. ___ 7. ___ 8. ___ 9. ___
10. ___ 11. ___ 12. ___ 13. ___ 14. ___ 15. ___

SCIENCE, HEALTH & TECHNOLOGY

file Datei **to file (s.th.)**
Transferring files is now easier than ever thanks to cloud storage and file-sharing.

to infiltrate eindringen in **infiltration** (n.); **infiltrator** (n.)
There have been many attempts to infiltrate the national computer network.

mobile (phone) (BE)/**cell phone** (AE) Handy
Sorry I missed your call, I didn't have my mobile with me.

on the Internet im Internet
Huge amounts of information can be found on the Internet today.

operating system Betriebssystem
Microsoft's Windows is one of the oldest operating systems around.

outdated veraltet; überholt
Technology becomes outdated very quickly these days.

programmable programmierbar **to program**
Computers are programmable to perform different tasks automatically.

programmer Programmierer
Steve Jobs was neither a hardware engineer nor a software programmer.

programming language Programmiersprache
An IT specialist must be able to write software code in different programming languages.

to release s.th. onto the market etw. auf den Markt bringen **release** (n.)
Almost every year, Apple releases a new iPhone onto the market.

to result in s.th. zu etw. führen **result** (n.)
Taking online quizzes can result in a lot of spam mail.

to secure sichern **security** (n.); **secure** (adj.)
It is important for companies to secure their networks against hackers.

SCIENCE, HEALTH & TECHNOLOGY

spreadsheet calculation Tabellenkalkulation
The Excel software allows you to produce spreadsheet calculations.

to store data Daten speichern **storage** (n.)
Data can be stored on hard drives, in data clouds online, or on USB flash drives.

to stream streamen **livestream** (n.)
Companies like Netflix and Amazon allow internet users to stream movies and series.

 85 *Solve the puzzle using words from these two pages.*

Across
1. Safe
3. Apps like Netflix allow you to do this with films and videos, so you can watch them on your computer or other device.
4. If you can't reach me under my home number, please try my _ _ _ _ _ _ .
5. To occur or follow as a consequence of s.th.
6. To make s.th. such as a computer game, a film or piece of music available to the public
7. The opposite of up-to-date
8. A collection of data on your computer
9. To keep electronic data on your computer or other device
10. A system of rules and symbols for writing computer programs

Down
2. If you have a computer you can use a spreadsheet to do this complicated _ _ _ _ _ _ _ _ _ _ _ .

173

SCIENCE, HEALTH & TECHNOLOGY

to swipe (auf dem Bildschirm) wischen
Swipe right to read more on the next page.

to synchronize/synchronise (BE) **devices** Geräte synchronisieren
Apple devices are easy to synchronize with each other.

tablet Tablet-PC
Some teachers use tablets in their lessons.

technological advance technologischer Fortschritt   **advanced** (adj.)
Farmers have been able to improve yields through technological advances.

transaction Transaktion
An online transaction allows users to buy things without having to go to a store.

to turn (the volume) up/down lauter/leiser stellen
All smartphones and tablets have buttons for turning the volume up and down.

via per; via; mit
Now you can order food via an app on your smartphone.

to be vulnerable (to s.th.)
anfällig -; verletzlich -; gefährdet sein   **vulnerability** (n.)
A computer is more vulnerable to viruses if it is not protected by special software.

wireless drahtlos; WLAN   **Wi-Fi**
Most airlines now offer wireless internet service.

word processing Textverarbeitung   **word processor** (n.)
You'll need to use a word processing program to write your report.

ROBOTICS

advance Fortschritt   **advancement** (n.); **advanced** (adj.)
Recent advances in technology enable robots to act more and more like humans.

SCIENCE, HEALTH & TECHNOLOGY

complex komplex; kompliziert **complexity** (n.)
Although robots usually perform simple tasks, robotic technology is very complex.

to explore s.th.
etw. erforschen **explorer** (n.); **exploration** (n.); **exploratory** (adj.)
Robotics is all about exploring new ways to make robots more useful for humans.

to launch a missile eine Rakete abschießen **launch** (n.)
Military drones will be able to launch missiles without human decision-making.

microsurgery Mikrochirurgie **surgeon** (n.); **surgical** (adj.)
Microsurgery is so complicated that some of it is performed using robotics.

? 86 *Find words on these two pages that match the definitions.*

1. A very small computer that doesn't have a separate keyboard or a mouse ____

2. To make the sound on a device louder ____

3. To shoot a missile into the sky ____

4. To make a movement with your hand on a mobile device; e.g. to get to the next page ____

5. Likely to be attacked or harmed ____

6. The production of text on a computer ____

7. Progress; a development or improvement ____

8. To examine or investigate s.th. in order to find out more about it ____

SCIENCE, HEALTH & TECHNOLOGY

to operate on s.o. jdn. operieren **operation** (n.)
Robotic tools are already being used to operate on certain patients.

to perform s.th. etw. durchführen **performance** (n.)
Robots can perform some difficult or repetitive tasks for humans.

remote control Fernbedienung; Fernsteuerung
Many robots cannot do much on their own and require a remote control to work.

remotely aus der Ferne **remote** (adj.)
Robots help perform dangerous jobs remotely without putting people in danger.

to do research forschen **to research; researcher** (n.)
Scientists and students at universities are doing lots of research on robots today.

SURVEILLANCE TECHNOLOGY

robot Roboter **robotic** (adj.)
A robot is a machine that can carry out a complex series of actions automatically.

CCTV (closed-circuit television) Videoüberwachung
CCTV is very common in the UK.

to combat bekämpfen **combat** (n.); **combatant** (n.; adj.)
Increased surveillance may be necessary to combat terrorism.

to detect s.th. etw. aufspüren; etw. entdecken **detection** (n.)
Dogs are much better at detecting drugs or explosives than humans.

facial recognition technology Gesichtserkennungstechnologie **to recognize**
Facial recognition technology can sometimes help to identify criminals.

to fingerprint Fingerabdrücke nehmen **fingerprint** (n.)
After 9/11, US airports started fingerprinting passengers.

SCIENCE, HEALTH & TECHNOLOGY

image enhancement Bildverbesserung **to enhance**
Digital image enhancement is one of the most important technologies for catching criminals.

internet traffic Internetverkehr
The software breaks up and sends users' internet traffic on multiple paths.

to locate orten **location** (n.)
GPS can help locate people via their smartphone.

to monitor s.th./s.o. etw./jdn. überwachen **monitor** (n.)
Some politicians say that the police should monitor potential terrorists at all times.

? 87 *Complete the sentences with words and expressions from these two pages.*

1. The supermarket uses _____ to stop people stealing goods.

2. Scientists used _____ to create better pictures of Mars.

3. If you have a smartphone, it is easy to _____ you wherever you are.

4. Smart gadgets let you control the temperature of your home _____ while you are still at the office.

5. The patient's heart, breathing and blood pressure were _____ during the operation.

6. _____ done by scientists all over the world shows that climate change is real.

7. With this test, we can _____ the disease at a much earlier stage.

8. Taylor Swift used _____ technology to detect stalkers at a concert in Los Angeles.

SCIENCE, HEALTH & TECHNOLOGY

to process s.th. etw. verarbeiten · **processor** (n.)
Surveillance data has to be processed before it can be used to catch criminals.

to record s.th. etw. aufnehmen · **recording** (n.)
The incident was recorded by several security cameras.

security camera Überwachungskamera
Public spaces are often watched on security cameras, so that people can feel safer there.

surveillance Überwachung
Many people are against surveillance of public spaces because they don't want to feel like they are being watched at all times.

surveillance footage Bildmaterial der Überwachungskameras
The police had to check the surveillance footage of more than 20 cameras.

to track s.o. jds. Spur verfolgen · **to lose track of s.o.**
The FBI used drones to track the murder suspect.

 88 Write the English word or expression in the space provided. All the words are on this page.

1. Überwachungskamera _____

2. jds. Spur verfolgen _____

3. etw. aufnehmen _____

4. etw. verarbeiten _____

5. Überwachung _____

6. Bildmaterial der Überwachungs- _____
   kameras

9 THE USA & THE UK  USA

melting pot Schmelztiegel   to melt
In the melting pot that is New York, many people speak two or more languages.

land of opportunity Land der unbegrenzten Möglichkeiten
America was seen by many immigrants as a land of opportunity.

Declaration of Independence Unabhängigkeitserklärung   to declare
Thomas Jefferson was the principal author of the Declaration of Independence.

founding fathers Gründerväter   to found; founder (n.)
Hamilton is a hip-hop musical about America's founding fathers.

liberty Freiheit   libertarian (adj.)
Religious liberty is an important topic in Utah, where many Mormons live.

pursuit of s.th. Streben nach etw.   to pursue
The Declaration of Independence includes the right to the pursuit of happiness.

amendment Änderung; Zusatz   to amend
The Second Amendment of the US Constitution allows adults to carry guns.

 THE BRITISH EMPIRE

to acquire s.th. etw. erwerben   acquisition (n.)
Britain acquired Germany's East and West African colonies in the Treaty of Versailles.

administration Verwaltung   to administer; administrator (n.)
The administration was undertaken by a relatively small number of officials.

the British Raj die britische Herrschaft in Indien
The British Raj ruled India for almost two centuries.

the Caribbean die Karibik
Jamaica and Trinidad are two of the Caribbean islands represented in London.

to colonize/colonise (BE) **a country** ein Land kolonisieren
Zimbabwe was colonised by Cecil Rhodes in the late 1800s.

colony Kolonie **colonial** (adj.)
There are not many signs that Nigeria was once a British colony.

to cover an area s. über ein Gebiet erstrecken **coverage** (n.)
By 1921, the British Empire covered an area of about 14.3 million square miles.

decolonization/decolonisation (BE) Entkolonisierung
African decolonisation started with the independence of countries such as Egypt.

89 *Complete the sentences with words and expressions from the word lists on this page and the next.*

1. The United States is often called a _____ because people of many cultures live there.
2. Everyone is supposed to have a chance to get to the top in the US; that's why it is known as the land of _____ .
3. _____ is such an important concept in the US that there is a very famous statue named after it.
4. The people who started the United States as a country and wrote the constitution are known as the _____ .
5. The first _____ of the US Constitution protects freedom of expression.
6. British rule in India was known as the _____ .
7. The Commonwealth has 53 members, most of them former British _____ .
8. Life, liberty and the _____ of happiness are rights according to the Declaration of Independence.

THE USA & THE UK

to expand s. erweitern; expandieren **expansion** (n.)
The empire expanded to include India, parts of Africa and many other territories.

to found s.th. etw. gründen **founder** (n.); **foundation** (n.)
The East India Company was founded to do trade with South and Southeast Asia.

to gain independence Unabhängigkeit erlangen **independent** (adj.)
Kenya gained independence from Britain in 1963.

to grant a country independence ein Land in die Unabhängigkeit entlassen
The Gold Coast became the first black African nation to be granted independence.

indigenous people; Aboriginal people (Australia) Ureinwohner
British colonisation was catastrophic for Indigenous Australians.

jewel Edelstein; Juwel **jewellery** (n.)
India was the jewel in the crown of the British Empire.

missionary Missionar(in) **mission** (n.)
David Livingstone was a missionary who wanted to introduce Africans to Christianity.

mistreatment schlechte Behandlung **to mistreat**
Aboriginal and Torres Strait Islander people suffered decades of mistreatment.

overseas settlement Siedlung in Übersee
Overseas settlements were established in North America and the West Indies.

partition Teilung **to partition**
Partition divided colonial India into two separate states: Pakistan and India.

protectorate Schutzherrschaft; Schutzgebiet
After the end of the British protectorate in 1961, Kuwait became independent.

to reign (over) herrschen (über) **reign** (n.)
Queen Victoria reigned from 1837 until her death in 1901.

THE USA & THE UK

to rule a country ein Land beherrschen **rule** (n.); **ruler** (n.)
For most of the 19th century, India was ruled by the British.

self-government Selbstverwaltung
In the 1950s, the British granted self-government and independence to some of their colonies.

sovereignty Oberhoheit; Souveränität **sovereign** (n.)
The Spanish government has called for joint sovereignty over Gibraltar following the Brexit vote.

90 *Use words and expressions from this page and the previous page to replace the underlined words in the sentences.*

1. India was so valuable to the British that it was known as the <u>precious stone</u> in the crown of the Empire. _____

2. The <u>splitting of India into two parts</u> resulted in an outbreak of terrible violence. _____

3. Queen Elizabeth I <u>ruled</u> England and Ireland for 45 years. _____

4. The Colony of Virginia was <u>established</u> in 1606. _____

5. <u>People who convert others to Christianity</u> were sent to South America by the Catholic Church. _____

6. The native people hoped that they would be given <u>the power to govern themselves</u>. _____

7. Canada did not <u>get</u> full independence until 1931. _____

to supply s.o. with s.th.   jdn. mit etw. versorgen   supply (n.); supplier (n.)
British companies supplied the colonies with slaves until 1807.

territory   Gebiet   territorial (adj.)
St Helena is Britain's second oldest overseas territory after Bermuda.

transition   Übergang
The transition to the Commonwealth is a great achievement of the monarchy.

THE COMMONWEALTH

association   Staatenbund   to be associated
The Commonwealth is an association of 52 independent and equal sovereign states.

common heritage   gemeinsames Erbe
Canada and Australia are linked by a shared outlook and common heritage.

to comprise   bestehen aus
The Commonwealth comprises 52 states that were mostly former British colonies.

declaration   Erklärung   to declare
In 1965, Rhodesia unilaterally declared independence.

dependency   abhängiges Gebiet
Jersey, Guernsey and the Isle of Man are Crown dependencies.

diversity   Vielfalt   diverse (adj.)
The Commonwealth contains a diversity of various cultures, races and languages.

former   ehemalig   formerly (adv.)
The former British colony of Australia wants Britain to stay in the European Union.

head   Oberhaupt   to head
The Queen is still head of the Church of England.

THE USA & THE UK

legislature Legislative; gesetzgebende Gewalt   **legislation** (n.); **legislative** (adj.)
The UK parliament is a legislature with two chambers: the House of Commons and the House of Lords.

monarchy Monarchie   **monarch** (n.)
The UK is a constitutional monarchy with Queen Elizabeth II as head of state.

sovereign Monarch; Herrscher
As the sovereign, the Queen is the UK head of state.

sovereign state unabhängiger Staat   **sovereignty** (n.)
The sovereign states in the Commonwealth were once part of the British Empire.

91 *Use the parts of words below to make words that replace the question marks.*

reign • versity • lature • heri • com • sove • tage • di • legis • prised

1. The USA and the UK share language and history; they have a common **?**.

2. In multicultural London, many people value the **?** of the city's population.

3. By 1783, the British Empire **?** colonies in Canada, America and the West Indies.

4. The UK's **?** is made up of the House of Commons and the House of Lords.

5. In the 18th century, George I was the elector of Hanover and also the British **?**.

Use the letters in the blue squares to find the word that means an area of land belonging to a country or person.

SOLUTIONS

TODAY'S SOCIETY

1
1. g • 2. e • 3. f • 4. a • 5. c • 6. i • 7. h • 8. j • 9. b • 10. d

2
1. marital • 2. only • 3. cliques • 4. same-sex • 5. stepmother • 6. single • 7. sibling • 8. separated

3
1. to lose one's temper • 2. to fend for oneself • 3. mood swing • 4. difference of opinion • 5. peer group • 6. to give s.o. advice • 7. driving licence (BE); driver's license (AE) • 8. to mature • 9. to moan about s.th./s.o. • 10. gap year

4
1. responsible • 2. pressure/pressurise • 3. rebellion • 4. sulky • 5. volunteer • 6. affordable • 7. charitable • 8. evicted

5
Across: 1. pursue • 3. spectator • 4. rented • 5. DIY • 6. rough • 7. shelter • 8. mass • 9. landlord • 10. shortage;
Down: 2. retirement

6
1. wavelength • 2. engaged • 3. spectator • 4. crush • 5. target • 6. break • 7. travel

7
1. heartbroken/brokenhearted • 2. strained • 3. hostile • 4. rowed • 5. make the first move • 6. atheists • 7. superficial

8
Bible, biblical • Christianity, Christian • to go to church, churchgoing • attendance • belief, believer, believable • to commit, committed • communal • baptism • confession, confessional

9
1. convert • 2. conscience • 3. devout • 4. heaven • 5. thought • 6. confirmation • 7. humanity | Person with extreme beliefs: **fanatic**

10
1. immoral • 2. justice • 3. national holiday • 4. mass • 5. monastery • 6. in private • 7. mosque • 8. miracle • 9. nonbeliever • 10. monk

11
1. o • 2. i • 3. g • 4. j • 5. d • 6. n • 7. b • 8. c • 9. f • 10. k • 11. l • 12. h • 13. a • 14. m • 15. e

12
1. inappropriately • 2. worship • 3. trustworthy • 4. public figure • 5. sermon • 6. emulate • 7. looks • 8. looked up

13
1. athletes • 2. challenging • 3. amateurish • 4. competitors • 5. disqualification • 6. advertisement/ad/advert • 7. champions • 8. earnings

14
1. endurance • 2. injury • 3. referee • 4. enhancing • 5. exercise • 6. exhaustion • 7. equipment

15
1. stadium • 2. thrill • 3. televised • 4. sample • 5. violence • 6. took up • 7. tournament • 8. measures

ECONOMY, GLOBALIZATION & TOURISM

❓ 16
Across: 1. discount • 3. borrow • 4. amount • 5. commerce • 6. afford • 7. account • 8. officer • 9. rate • 10. consultant; **Down:** 2. commercial

❓ 17
1. market share • 2. to subsidise/subsidize • 3. to take out a loan • 4. profit • 5. range • 6. interest rate • 7. retail • 8. to lend money • 9. human resources • 10. to undercut

❓ 18
1. c • 2. f • 3. d • 4. g • 5. j • 6. k • 7. o • 8. b • 9. n • 10. l • 11. a • 12. m • 13. h • 14. i • 15. e

❓ 19
1. Depression • 2. downturn • 3. growth • 4. unemployment benefit/benefits • 5. gross domestic product/GDP • 6. essentials • 7. income • 8. economic and monetary union

❓ 20
1. manufacturing • 2. poverty • 3. prosperity • 4. merger • 5. property • 6. inflation | American English expression: **real estate**

❓ 21
1. stock market • 2. starving • 3. skilled labour • 4. tariffs • 5. developing countries • 6. unemployment • 7. customs

❓ 22
Across: 1. spread • 3. citizenship • 4. origin • 5. asylum • 6. barrier • 7. relocate • 8. WTO • 9. seeker; **Down:** 2. assimilate

❓ 23
1. detention • 2. to deport s.o. • 3. to flee a country • 4. to emigrate • 5. famine • 6. illegal immigrant • 7. influx • 8. custom • 9. foreigner • 10. descendant

❓ 24
1. residence • 2. restricted • 3. settlers • 4. backpacking • 5. conservation • 6. skier • 7. transition • 8. settlement

❓ 25
1. f • 2. m • 3. h • 4. i • 5. k • 6. o • 7. a • 8. d • 9. l • 10. b • 11. n • 12. j • 13. g • 14. c • 15. e

❓ 26
1. operator • 2. transportation • 3. agency/agent • 4. resort • 5. sports facilities • 6. relax • 7. profited • 8. absenteeism

❓ 27
1. (their) employees • 2. dismissal • 3. collaborate • 4. discrimination • 5. co-workers • 6. competitors • 7. blue-collar workers • 8. downsized

❓ 28
1. grievances • 2. equal opportunity • 3. security • 4. livelihood • 5. application • 6. notice • 7. freelance

❓ 29
1. to make a living • 2. to promote • 3. manufacturing process • 4. minimum wage • 5. overtime • 6. part-time • 7. pay rise/pay raise • 8. to take maternity/paternity/parental leave • 9. to negotiate with s.o. • 10. pension plan

SOLUTIONS

❓ 30
1. redundancies • 2. replacement • 3. promoted • 4. salaried • 5. retirement • 6. recruiter • 7. shares • 8. strikers

❓ 31
Across: 2. workforce • 5. trade • 8. worker • 9. white-collar • 10. fire • 11. apprentice • 12. union • 13. manual; Down: 1. retire • 3. overtime • 4. supervisor • 6. wage • 7. vocational | IT company: **Microsoft**

EDUCATION

❓ 32
1. tuition fee • 2. financial aid • 3. vocational qualifications • 4. higher education • 5. distance learning • 6. degree courses

❓ 33
1. acquired • 2. attend • 3. gained • 4. revise • 5. achieve • 6. assessed • 7. hands-on • 8. illiterate

❓ 34
1. boarding school • 2. coeducational/co-ed • 3. to drop out of school • 4. compulsory education • 5. primary school (BE)/ elementary school (AE) • 6. to bully s.o. • 7. to be eligible for s.th. • 8. comprehensive school • 9. to cheat • 10. to take a course

❓ 35
Across: 1. grade • 2. formal • 3. mark • 4. independent • 5. curricular • 6. exchange • 7. entrance • 8. senior • 9. junior • 10. infant; Down: 1. graduation

❓ 36
1. c • 2. e • 3. f • 4. h • 5. k • 6. n • 7. b • 8. l • 9. j • 10. o • 11. m • 12. d • 13. i • 14. g • 15. a

❓ 37
Across: 3. fail • 7. fee • 9. cheat • 10. library • 11. illiterate • 12. scholarship • 13. tuition • 14 sex; Down: 1. major • 2. humanities • 4. report • 5. degree • 6. bully • 8. drop out | University: **Cambridge**

GOVERNMENT, LAW & POLITICS

❓ 38
1. demonstrators • 2. equal • 3. free • 4. oppressors • 5. refusal • 6. just • 7. prejudice • 8. involvement

❓ 39
abuse, abuser, abusive • accidental • admission • to allege, alleged • assassin, assassination • segregation, to segregate • to acquit • bribe, to bribe • accusation, accuser

❓ 40
1. capital punishment/the death penalty; committed • 2. confessed • 3. burglary • 4. charged • 5. community • 6. convicted • 7. abuse • 8. defendant

❓ 41
1. forgery • 2. evidence • 3. enforce • 4. firearm • 5. execution • 6. violence • 7. access | Not guilty = innocent

❓ 42
1. mugged • 2. homicide • 3. innocent • 4. imprisonment • 5. harassing • 6. lethal injection • 7. investigation • 8. offence/offense

SOLUTIONS

❓ 43
1. rape • 2. to plead guilty • 3. to seize s.th. • 4. to sentence s.o. to death • 5. penalty • 6. probation • 7. to put s.o. on trial • 8. to prove s.o.'s innocence • 9. to release s.o. from prison • public prosecutor/prosecuting attorney

❓ 44
1. solitary confinement • 2. suspect • 3. weapons • 4. hostages • 5. testified • 6. victims • 7. drug trafficking • 8. served her sentence

❓ 45
1. b • 2. d • 3. e • 4. j • 5. c • 6. f • 7. h • 8. g • 9. i • 10. a

❓ 46
Across: 1. defence/defense • 3. deliver • 4. consent • 5. citizen • 6. constituent • 7. force • 8. enshrine • 9. campaign • 10. duty • 11. delay; **Down:** 2. electorate

❓ 47
1. overall majority • 2. impeach • 3. govern • 4. impose • 5. foreign policy • 6. established • 7. general election

❓ 48
1. ratified • 2. polling stations • 3. pledged • 4. landslide • 5. opponents • 6. legislation • 7. member states • 8. intervened

❓ 49
1. social security • 2. supreme court • 3. to sign a treaty • 4. to represent s.o. • 5. tax • 6. to resign • 7. successor • 8. to swear an oath • 9. to swear s.o. in • 10. to respond to s.th.

❓ 50
1. g • 2. o • 3. n • 4. f • 5. i • 6. a • 7. e • 8. c • 9. j • 10. k • 11. m • 12. b • 13. l • 14. h • 15. d

❓ 51
1. h • 2. f • 3. e • 4. c • 5. d • 6. g • 7. a • 8. b

❓ 52
1. legislative • 2. Secretary • 3. judicial • 4. uphold • 5. primary • 6. nominee • 7. inauguration | Document: **constitution**

❓ 53
1. armed • 2. bear arms • 3. casualties • 4. committed • 5. ceasefire • 6. weapons • 7. act • 8. defeat

❓ 54
1. negotiated • 2. occupiers • 3. surrendered • 4. hostile • 5. wounded • 6. invaders • 7. survivors • 8. massacred

LITERATURE

❓ 55
1. eloquent • 2. climax • 3. to be set in/to take place in • 4. character • 5. denouement • 6. to deal with s.th./s.o. • 7. to imagine s.th. • 8. to undergo a change • 9. to address s.th. to s.o. • 10. to feature

❓ 56
Across: 1. pun • 2. first-person • 3. heroine • 4. imagery • 5. personification • 6. omniscient • 7. devices • 8. plot; **Down:** 1. protagonist

❓ 57
1. f • 2. i • 3. j • 4. b • 5. l • 6. m • 7. d • 8. c • 9. k • 10. e • 11. h • 12. a • 13. n • 14. g

SOLUTIONS

❓ 58
1. e • 2. c • 3. b • 4. a • 5. f • 6. d • 7. h • 8. g

❓ 59
1. rehearse • 2. soliloquies • 3. blank verse • 4. Rhyming couplets • 5. script • 6. stage • 7. stanzas

MEDIA

❓ 60
1. attention-grabbing • 2. advertise • 3. classified ads • 4. colour supplement • 5. deception • 6. revenue • 7. appeals • 8. market research

❓ 61
1. audio file • 2. to create • 3. to have access to s.th. • 4. digital subscription • 5. online audience • 6. to enter s.th. • 7. to bookmark a website • 8. on the net/internet • 9. keyword • 10. digital age

❓ 62
1. secure • 2. circulated • 3. search term • 4. private • 5. search engine • 6. editorial • 7. spread • 8. columnists

❓ 63
1. letter to the editor • 2. obituary • 3. periodicals • 4. popular; readership • 5. quality • 6. subscription fee • 7. tabloids • 8. copyright

❓ 64
1. covers • 2. biased • 3. censored • 4. came under fire • 5. current affairs • 6. critic • 7. factual

❓ 65
gossip, gossip column, gossipy • invader, to invade, invasive • misleading • publication, publisher • review, to review • satire, satirist, satirical • issue • quote, quotation • journalism, journalistic

❓ 66
Across 1. cable • 3. break • 4. episode • 5. sensationalist • 6. media • 7. documentary • 8. news • 9. contestant; Down 2. broadcast

❓ 67
1. spreading • 2. have • 3. search • 4. bookmarked • 5. misled • 6. carried • 7. created • 8. post • 9. surfing • 10. censored • 11. broadcast • 12. enter • 13. published • 14. personalise

❓ 68
1. accommodation • 2. commuters • 3. development • 4. crowded • 5. public transport • 6. inhabitants/residents • 7. preserve them • 8. congestion

❓ 69
1. to surround s.th. • 2. tower block • 3. biodegradable • 4. urbanisation/urbanization • 5. rush hour • 6. adverse effect • 7. rural • 8. on the brink of extinction • 9. to avert s.th. • 10. residential area

❓ 70
1. consumption • 2. contribution • 3. destruction • 4. disastrous • 5. disposal • 6. emissions • 7. conserve • 8. devastation

❓ 71
1. d • 2. e • 3. g • 4. j • 5. l • 6. b • 7. n • 8. k • 9. f • 10. o • 11. m • 12. i • 13. a • 14. h • 15. c

SOLUTIONS

❓ 72
1. hurricane • 2. pesticide • 3. landfill •
• 4. packaging • 5. irreversible • 6. incinerator
• 7. organic

❓ 73
1. to recycle • 2. precipitation • 3. renewable
• 4. to be at risk of extinction • 5. sewage
treatment plant • 6. poison • 7. to pollute
• 8. skin cancer • 9. power station/plant •
10. ray

❓ 74
1. arid • 2. soil • 3. sustainable • 4. species
• 5. sort (our) rubbish • 6. target • 7. toxic

❓ 75
1. English Channel; cliffs • 2. fertile •
3. desert • 4. countryside • 5. cover an area
• 6. lush • 7. county • 8. Highlands

❓ 76
1. natural disaster • 2. temperate • 3. prairie
• 4. wilderness • 5. coast • 6. mountainous •
7. marshy • 8. plain

SCIENCE, HEALTH & TECHNOLOGY

❓ 77
1. conducted • 2. modified • 3. crops •
4. cured • 5. defective • 6. determine
• 7. decode • 8. disorders

❓ 78
1. infertile • 2. long-/short-term effect •
3. malformation • 4. lab; laboratory
• 5. mammal • 6. organ donor • 7. herbicide
resistant • 8. pest • 9. insemination •
10. to inherit s.th. from s.o.

❓ 79
1. researching • 2. yield • 3. stem • 4. raises
• 5. screened • 6. transplanted • 7. rejecting
• 8. vaccinated

❓ 80
1. addictive • 2. allergic • 3. approach •
4. burden • 5. contraception/birth control
• 6. risk • 7. ache • 8. ageing; benefits

❓ 81
1. disorder • 2. decline • 3. dignity •
4. contagious • 5. elderly • 6. eradication
• 7. condition | Doctor who performs
operations: **surgeon**

❓ 82
1. b • 2. c • 3. a • 4. g • 5. i • 6. d • 7. f • 8. e
• 9. j • 10. h

❓ 83
1. pregnancy • 2. obesity • 3. nausea •
4. to prescribe • 5. residential care • 6. to
neglect • 7. to overdo • 8. slight/elevated
temperature • 9. runny nose • 10. screening

❓ 84
1. e • 2. c • 3. i • 4. n • 5. g • 6. b • 7. k • 8. o
• 9. m • 10. l • 11. d • 12. a • 13. j • 14. h • 15. f

❓ 85
Across: 1. secure • 3. stream • 4. mobile
• 5. result • 6. release • 7. outdated •
8. file • 9. store • 10. language
Down: 2. calculation

❓ 86
1. tablet • 2. to turn (the volume) up
• 3. to launch • 4. to swipe • 5. vulnerable •
6. word processing • 7. advance •
8. to explore

SOLUTIONS

❓ 87
1. CCTV/closed-circuit television • 2. image enhancement • 3. locate • 4. remotely • 5. monitored • 6. Research • 7. detect • 8. facial recognition

❓ 88
1. security camera • 2. to track s.o. • 3. to record s.th. • 4. to process s.th. • 5. surveillance • 6. surveillance footage

THE USA & THE UK

❓ 89
1. melting pot • 2. opportunity • 3. Liberty • 4. Founding Fathers • 5. amendment • 6. British Raj • 7. colonies • 8. pursuit

❓ 90
1. jewel • 2. partition of India • 3. reigned over • 4. founded • 5. Missionaries • 6. sovereignty • 7. gain

❓ 91
1. heritage • 2. diversity • 3. comprised • 4. legislature • 5. sovereign
Area of land: **territory**

🇬🇧 BRITISH AND AMERICAN ENGLISH

Here are the main differences between British and American English spellings.

1. Words ending in **–re** in British English (BE) end in **–er** in American English (AE).
   centre (BE); **center** (AE) • **theatre** (BE); **theater** (AE)

2. Words ending in **–our** in BE end in **–or** in AE.
   colour (BE); **color** (AE) • **humour** (BE); **humor** (AE)

3. Words ending in **–ize** or **–ization** are a little more complicated. The endings **–ize** and **–ization** are acceptable in both BE and AE, but **–ise** and **–isation** are only correct in BE. In your own writing you should choose one spelling and stick to it.
   organize, organise (BE); **organize** (AE) • **realization, realisation** (BE); **realization** (AE)

4. Words that end in a **vowel plus l** are doubled before endings in BE. In AE they are not doubled.
   to travel, travelled (BE); **traveled** (AE) • **to revel, reveller** (BE); **reveler** (AE)

5. Words that are spelled with **ae** or **oe** in BE are just spelled with **e** in AE.
   foetus (BE); **fetus** (AE) • **paediatrician** (BE); **pediatrician** (AE)

6. Words that end in **–ence** in BE end in **–ense** in AE.
   defence (BE); **defense** (AE) • **offence** (BE); **offense** (AE)

7. Words that end in **–ogue** in BE end in **–og** in AE.
   catalogue (BE); **catalog** (AE) • **dialogue** (BE); **dialog** (BE)

INDEX

A

A levels/Advanced levels 69
abolish 91
Aboriginal 181
abortion 162
absenteeism 54
abuse 80
access 124
accession 91
accident 80
accommodation 138
account 34
accountant 34
accuse 80
ache 162
achieve one's potential 68
acquire 179
acquire skills 68
acquit 80
act 119
act of war 108
actor/actress 119
ad/advert/advertisement 54
addict 162
address 112
administration 104; 179
admit 80
adolescence 6
adopt 4
adult 7
advance 174
adventure 28
adverse effect 140
advertise 122; 28
advertising campaign 122
advice column 126
advocate 92
affairs 92
affirmative action 54
afford 34
affordable 10
age 162
agreement 92
agriculture 55
allegation 80
allergy 162
alliteration 112
ally 92
amateur 28
ambassador 92
amend 92
amendment 179
amount 34
Anglican 17

anorexia 162
answer back 7
appeal 122
apply for a job 55
appoint 92
appointment 161
apprentice 55
apprenticeship 66
approach 162
approve 92
archbishop 17
argue 16
arid 151
armed forces 108
arrest 80
ask out 14
assassination 80
assault 80
assembly 69
assembly line 55
assess 68
assimilate 46
association 183
assonance 113
asylum 46
asylum seeker 46
atheist 17
athlete 31
athletics 28
atmosphere 113
attack 170
attend a religious service 17
attend school 69
attention-grabbing 122
attorney 81
Attorney General 104
audio file 124
austerity measures 38
authenticate 170
avert 140

B

backpacking 50
bailout package 38
balanced diet 162
ball games 28
ballot 92
ballot box 92
ban 28; 92
bankrupt 38
baptise 18
basic requirement 56
BBC 134
bear arms 108

beat a record 28
behave inappropriately 26
belief 18
beneficial 162
biased 130
Bible 18
bill 93
biodegradable 140
birth 162
birth control 162
birth rate 163
bishop 18
blank verse 120
blue-collar worker 56
boarding school 70
bombing 81
book in advance 51
bookmark a website 124
boom 38
boost growth 38
border (on) 151
border control 47
border/frontier 152
borrow money 34
brand 122
break a law 81
break a record 28
break it off 14
breaking news 130
breed 156
bribe 81
brink of extinction 141
British Broadcasting
  Corporation 134
British Isles 152
British Raj 179
broadcast 134
broadcasting company 134
brokenhearted 16
Buddhism 18
budget 38
bulimia 163
bully 70
burden on society 163
burglary 82
business 34
business district 138
by-election 102

C

cable TV 134
calculation 170
candidate 106
canyon 152

192

INDEX

capital 38
capital punishment 82
carbon dioxide 141
career 56
Caribbean 180
carry 122
cast 119
cast a vote 93
casualty 108
catch (a) cold 164
Catholic 18
caucus 104
CCTV 176
ceasefire 108
cell phone 172
censor 130
CEO 34
CFCs 141
challenge 28
chamber 104
championship 28
Chancellor of the Exchequer 102
character 113
charge with a crime 82
charity 11
cheat 70
checks and balances 93
chemical weapon 108
chief executive officer 34
child abuse 82
child care 4
chlorofluorocarbons 141
Christian 18
Christian values 18
church attendance 18
Church of England 18
churchgoer 18
circulation 126
citizen 94
citizenship 47
citizenship test 47
civil disobedience 78
civil liberties 78
civil rights movement 78
civil war 108
civilian 108
claim/collect unemployment benefit(s) 40
clash 28
classic 112
classified ad 122
cliff 152
climate change 141

climax 113
clique 7
close 14
closed-circuit television 176
CO_2 141
coast 154
co-educational/co-ed 70
cohabit 4
collaborate 56
collateral 34
college 66
colonise/colonize a country 180
colony 180
colour supplement 122
column 126
combat 176
combat sports 28
come down with s.th. 166
come under fire 130
comedy 116
commander-in-chief 104
commerce 34
commercial 134
commercial break 134
commercial TV 134
commit a crime 82
commit atrocities 108
commitment 19
committed 94
common heritage 183
communicate 124
communion 19
community 19
community service 82
commuter 138
compassion 26
competition 29
competitive 56
complex 175
comprehensive school 70
comprise 183
compulsory education 70
condition 164
conduct 156
confess 82
confession 19
confirmation 20
congestion 138
Congress 104
connectivity 124
conscience 20
conscription 108
consent 94

conservation 142
conserve 51
constituent 94
Constitution 104
constitutional monarchy 102
consultant 34
consume 38; 142
consumer goods 34
consumer spending 38
contagious 164
contaminate 142
contestant 134
contraception 162
contract 56
contribute 142
controversial 130; 156
convention 104
convert 20
convict 82
copy 70
copyright 128
core subject 70
cosmopolitan 138
cough 164
council 138
country of origin 47
countryside 152
county 152
couple 4
course 70
coursework 70
cover 130
cover an area 152; 180
cover letter 59
co-worker 56
craftsman/-woman 56
crash 170
create 124
credit crunch 38
criminal 82
criminal law 82
criminal offence/offense 82
crisis 38
critic 130
criticize/criticise 7
crop 156
cross species 156
cross-country skiing 51
crossword puzzle 127
crowded 138
cruise 51
cure 156
current affairs 131
curriculum 70

193

INDEX

curriculum vitae (CV) 56
custodial sentence 82
custody 5
custom 48
customs 44
cut taxes 38
CV 56
cyberbullying 83

D

data theft 170
database 170
deadly 164
deal 112
debt 39
deception 122
declaration 183
Declaration of Independence 104; 179
declare s.th. unconstitutional 104
declare war 108
decline 164
decode 156
decolonisation/ decolonization 180
decrease 39
Deep South 78
defeat 109
defective gene 156
defence/defense 94
defend 83
defendant 83
deforestation 142
degree course 66
delay 94
delay starting a family 4
delegate 104
delinquent 84
deliver a speech 94
delivery time 56
demand 39
demonstration 78
denouement 113
Department for/ of Education 70
dependency 183
deport 48
descendant 48
describe 114
desert 152
design 124; 171
destination 52
destruction 142

detect 176
detective novel 116
detention 48
detergent 142
determine 156
devastating effect 142
developing country 45
development 138
device 171
devout 20
diet 164
difference of opinion 8
digital age 124
digital subscription 124
dignity 164
diploma 66
disarmament 109
disaster 142
discount 35
discrimination 56
disease 142; 156
dismissal 57
disposable income 12
dispose of 142
disqualify 29
distance learning 66
district 152
diverse 4
diversity 183
divorce 4
documentary 134
do-it-yourself (DIY) 12
domestic violence 84
download 171
downsize 57
draft 108
drama 116
dramatist 119
driving licence/ driver's license 8
drop out of school 71
drought 142
duty 94

E

earn one's living 29
eating disorder 164
economic and monetary union 40
economic downturn 40
economic growth 40
economic migrant 48
economy 40
ecotourism 52

edition 129
editor 131
editorial 127
efficient 40
elderly 164
elect 94
election campaign 94
electoral college 105
electorate 95
elementary school 71
eligible 71
eligible to vote 93
eliminate 95
eloquent 112
emigrate 48
emissions 143
emit 143
employ 57
employee 57
emulate 26
endangered species 143
endurance 30
energy-efficient 144
enforce a law 84
engaged 14
English Channel 152
enjoy s.o.'s company 14
enshrine 95
enter 124
enter a new phase 8
entrance exam 72
environment 144
environmentally conscious 52
environmentally friendly 144
epidemic 164
episode 135
equal opportunity 58
equality 78
equipment 30
eradication 164
espionage 84
essentials 40
establish 96
European single market 40
European sovereign debt crisis 40
evangelical 20
evening class 68
eviction 11
evidence 84
examiner 68
exceed 144
exchange rate 35
exchange student 72

INDEX

execution 84
executive branch 105
exercise 30; 165
exhaust fumes 144
exhaustion 30
expand 96; 181
expel 48
explore 52; 175
exposition 114
extended family 4
extra-curricular activity 72
extremism 20

F
fable 117
facial recognition technology 176
factual 131
fail an exam 72
fairy tale 117
faith 20
fall victim 84
famine 48
fanatic 20
fancy 14
favourable terms 35
feature 112; 171
feel under the weather 165
fend 8
fertile 152
fertilizer/fertiliser 144
fetus 165
fictional/fictitious 117
file 172
file for divorce 4
financial aid 66
financial crisis 40
fine 84
fingerprint 176
fire 62
firearm 84
first-past-the-post system 102
first-person narrator 114
fixed rules 30
flee a country 48
flooding 144
flu 166
foetus 165
food chain 144
force 94
forced labour 58
foreign affairs 102
foreign policy 96
foreign secretary 102

foreigner 48
forgery 84
form a government 102
formal education 72
former 183
fossil fuel 144
foster child/parents 4
found 35; 96; 181
founding fathers 179
fragile 52
fraud 84
free time 12
free trade 45
freedom 78
freedom of the press 131
freedom of thought 20
freelance 58
freshman 72
front line 109
front page 127
fuel 144
full-time 60
fund 96
fundamentalist 20

G
gain access 84
gain independence 181
gain knowledge 68
gain work experience 8
gap year 8
gay 4
GCSE 72
GDP 41
gene 156
General Certificate of Secondary Education 72
genetic disorder 157
genetic test 157
genetically modified 157
genre 117
get on well 15
give a speech 94
give advice 8
glacier 144
global trade 45
globalisation/globalization 45
GM 157
go down with s.th. 166
go on a date with s.o. 15
go out with s.o. 15
go through s.th. 8
go to war 109
goods 40

gossip 132
govern 96
governor 105
grade 72
graduation 72
grant a country independence 181
graphics 124
Great Depression 41
grievance 58
gross domestic product 41
groundwater 145
grow 52
growth 58
guide 52
guilty 85
gun control 85
gun ownership 85

H
habitat 145
hack 86
half-brother/-sister 5
hand in one's notice 58
hands-on experience 68
hang out 8
harass 86
hardback/hardcover 129
harmful 145
have a crush 15
have a negative impact 52
have a say 96
head 183
head 96
head of state 96
head teacher 72
headline 127
heal 157
health care 166
heartbroken 16
heatwave 145
heaven 20
hell 21
herbicide resistant 158
hereditary illness 166
hero/heroine 114
high school 69
higher education 66
highlands 152
hijack 86
hiking 52
hold an election 96
holy 21
home secretary 102

195

INDEX

homeland 48
homeless 11
homicide 86
hostage 90
hostel 11
hostile 16
hostilities 110
house arrest 88
House of Commons 102
House of Lords 103
House of Representatives 105
household 5
housing 138
housing shortage 12
human reproductive
    cloning 158
human resources 36
human trafficking 46
humanities 66
humanity 21
hurricane 146
hymn 21

I

iambic pentameter 120
ice sheet 146
identify 112
illegal immigrant 48
illiterate 68
image enhancement 177
imagery 114
imagine 112
immigration policy 49
immoral 22
immune system 166
impact 146
impeach 97
impersonal 16
implant 158
impose sanctions 97
imprisonment 86
improve one's performance 30
in private 22
in vitro fertilisation 158
inaugurate 106
incinerator 146
income 41
increase 41
independent school 72
indigenous people 181
individual 30
industrialisation/
    industrialization 58

industrialized nation 46
infant school 72
infect 166
infectious disease 166
infertile 158
infiltrate 172
inflation 42
influence 97
influenza 166
influx 49
infrastructure 42
inhabitant 138
inherit 158
injury 30
inland 153
innocent 86
insemination 158
intelligence 110
interest rate 36
internet 172
internet traffic 177
intervene 98
interview 58
intimate 16
invade 132
invasion 110
investigation 86
investment 42
involved 78
irreversible 146
issue 132
IVF 158

J

jail 86
Jew 22
jewel 181
job creation 58
job security 58
journalist 132
judge 86
judicial branch 106
junior 72
junior high school 73
junior school 73
justice 22; 78

K

keyword 124
kidnap 86
Koran 22

L

lab(oratory) 158
labor union 64
labour/labor 58
land of opportunity 179
landfill 146
landlord 12
landslide victory 98
launch 98
launch a missile 175
lawyer 81
lay off 58
legend 118
legislation 98
legislative branch 106
legislature 184
leisure industry 12
leisure time 12
lend money 36
lesbian 5
lethal injection 86
letter of application 59
letter to the editor 128
liberty 179
library 68
licence 170
life expectancy 166
lift sanctions 97
line 120
linguistic device 114
litter 146
livelihood 59
living conditions 138
living standard 42
loan 36
local community 52
locate 177
located 154
logging 146
loneliness 166
longevity 166
long-term care 166
long-term care insurance 167
long-term effect 158
look up to 26
looks 27
lose one's temper 8
love 14
love at first sight 16
low-income 12
lush 153
Lutheran 22
luxury flat 139
lyrical 120

INDEX

M
machinery 59
major 66
make a living 60
make the first move 16
malformation 158
malnutrition 167
mammal 158
manslaughter 86
manual skill 60
manufacturing 42
manufacturing process 60
marital problem 6
mark 73
market research 122
market share 36
marriage 6
marry 6
marshy 154
mass 22
mass entertainment 13
mass immigration 49
mass media 135
mass tourism 52
massacre 110
mass-produce 60
maternity leave 60
mature 8
measles 167
media industry 129
media landscape 129
medicine 167
melting pot 179
Member of Parliament 103
member of staff 74
member state 98
merchandise 36
merger 42
metre 120
microsurgery 175
military 110
military service 8
minimum wage 60
minority 50
miracle 22
mislead 132
mission 22
missionary 181
mistreatment 181
moan 9
mobile 172
mock exam 74
modify 158
monarchy 184

monastery 22
monitor 177
monk 22
monopoly 36
mood swing 9
Mormon 22
mortality 168
mosque 23
motor sports 30
mountain range 154
mountainous 154
moving 118
MP 103
mug 87
murder 87
mutation 159

N
narrative perspective 114
narrative prose 118
narrative technique 114
narrator 114
national curriculum 74
national holiday 23
national security 110
native 53
natural disaster 154
natural resources 146
naturalisation/naturalization 50
nausea 168
neglect 168
negotiate 60
negotiation 110
net 125
news 135
news source 132
newspaper article 128
nominee 106
nonbeliever 23
non-fiction 118
north 153; 154
novel 118
novelist 118
nuclear power 146
nun 24
nursery/nursery school 74

O
obesity 168
obey 30
obituary 128
objective 132
observance 24

occupy 110
offence/offense 87
Office for Standards in Education 74
oil spill 146
omniscient narrator 114
one-sided 132
online 170
online audience 125
only child 6
operate 176
operating system 172
opponent 98
oppression 78
oral examination 74
organ donor 159
organic farming 146
outdated 172
outsource 60
overall majority 96
overcrowding 139
overdo 168
overseas settlement 181
overtime 60
ozone layer 147

P – Q
package tour 53
packaging 147
paperback 130
parable 118
parental leave 60
partition 181
part-time 60
pass a law 98
pass an exam 68
passport 50
passport control 53
paternity leave 60
pay rise/pay raise 60
peer group 9
penalty 88
pension plan 61
perceptive 132
perform a task 74; 176
performance-enhancing drug 30
period 74
periodical 128
permanent residency 50
permanent resident 50
persecution 24
personalize/personalise 122
personification 114

197

INDEX

personnel 61
pest 159
pesticide 147
piracy 88
place an ad 123
plain 154
plateau 154
play truant 74
playwright 119
plead guilty 88
pledge 98
pledge of allegiance 24
plot 115
poem 118
point of view 115
poison 148
policy 98
politically impartial/
   neutral 103
politician 98
polling station 98
pollutant 148
pollute 148
pollution 148
Pope 24
popular 130
popular newspaper 128
popularity 53
population 98
pornography 125
post 125
poverty 42
POW 110
power 94
power station/plant 148
practice 24
prairie 154
prayer 24
preach 24
precipitation 148
pregnancy 168
prejudice 78
prescribe 168
preserve 139
pressure 10
priest 24
primary 106
primary education 74
primary school 71
principal 74
prison 86
prisoner of war 110
privacy 126
probation 88

process 178
producer 135
profession 61
profit 36; 54
programmable 172
programme/program 136
programmer 172
programming language 172
promote 61; 99
promotion 62
property 43
prose (fiction) 118
prosecutor/prosecuting
   attorney 88
prosperity 42
protagonist 115
protect 30; 148
protectorate 181
protest 79
Protestant 24
prove 88
provide a grant 36
puberty 10
public 99
public figure 27
public school 74
public sector broadcaster 136
public transport (system) 139
publish 132
pun 115
pursue an interest 13
pursuit of s.th. 179
push to the limits 31
put on trial 88
put under pressure 10
qualifications 66
quality newspaper 128
Quran 22
quote/quotation 132

R

race 31
racial tension 79
raise a moral concern 160
raise 42
raise standards 75
raise taxes 42
rally 79
range 36
rape 88
ratify a treaty 99
raw material 42
ray 148
readership 128

real estate 43
rebel 10
reception 75
recession 43
record 75; 178
recover 148
recruit 62
recycle 148
reduce a sentence 88
reduce poverty 43
redundant 62
ref(eree) 31
refugee 50
refuse 79
regulate 123
rehearse 120
reign 181
reject 160
relationship 16
relax 54
release from prison 88
release onto the market 172
religious affiliation 24
religious belief 25
religious denomination 25
relocate 46
remote control 176
remotely 176
renewable 148
rented accomodation 12
replace 62
report 132
report/report card 76
represent 100
reproduction 160
reputation 76
research 176
resident 138
residential area 140
residential care 168
resign 100
resistance 160
resolution 116
resort 54
respond 100
restriction 50
result 172
resumé 56
retail 36
retire 62
retirement 13
retrain 62
revenue 123
review 133

INDEX

revise 68
rhyme scheme 120
rhyming couplet 121
rhythm 121
rifle 88
risk 162
risk of extinction 149
robot 176
row 16
rule 182
rumour/rumor 133
run for president 106
running mate 106
runny nose 168
rural 140
rush hour 140

S

sack 62
sacred 25
safety gear 32
salary 62
same-sex marriage 6
SAT 76
satellite dish 136
satirical 133
scene 120
scholarship 66
Scholastic Assessment Test 76
screen for a disease 160
screening 168
script 120
sea level 151
sea level 149
search engine 126
search term 126
secondary education 76
secondary school 76
Secretary of Defense 106
Secretary of State 106
Secretary of the Interior 106
sectarian 25
section 128
secular 26
secure 126; 172
security 89
security camera 178
segregation 80
seize 89
self-government 182
semi-skilled 62
Senate 106
senior 62; 72
senior high school 69

sensationalist 134
sentence to death 89
separate 6
separation of church and state 26
sequence of events 116
series 136
sermon 26
serve a sentence 90
serve a term 100
service industry 37
service 130
set in 112
set of values 26
set up a business 62
set up on one's own 10
setting 116
settle 50
settle down 10
sewage treatment plant 149
share 43
shareholder 63
shelter 12
short-term effect 158
sibling rivalry 6
sick leave 63
side effect 168
sign a treaty 100
single 16
single currency 44
single parent 6
single-sex 76
sit an exam 76
situated 154
sixth form 76
skills 44
skilled labour/worker(s) 44
skills shortage 63
skin cancer 149
skip school 74
sleep rough 12
slope 154
smuggle 90
sneeze 169
soap (opera) 136
soar 37
social media 126
social security 100
soil 150
soil erosion 150
soldier 110
soliloquy 120
solitary confinement 90
sonnet 118

sophomore 72
sore throat 169
sort rubbish 150
south 153; 154
sovereign 184
sovereign state 184
sovereignty 182
spare time 12
speaker 103
special educational needs 76
species 150
spectator 13
spectator sport 14
spend 44
spiritual 26
sport/sports 29
sporting event 32
sports facilities 54
sports tourism 54
sportsman/sportswoman 32
sportswear 32
spread 46; 126
spreadsheet calculation 173
stadium 32
stage 120
stanza 121
starve 44
stem 160
stem cell research 160
stepbrother/-sister/-father/
 -mother 6
stimulant 90
stimulus package 44
stock 43; 150
stock market 44
stockholder 63
store data 173
strained 16
stream 173
strike 63
struggle 80
stylistic device 116
subject 76; 116
subscription fee 128
subsidise/subsidize 37
substitute teacher 76
subtitle 136
subway 140
successor 100
suffer 169
sulk 10
superficial 16
supervisor 64
supplier 64

199

INDEX

supply 183
supply teacher 76
supreme court 100
surf the Internet 126
surface 150
surrender 110
surrogate mother 160
surround 140
surveillance 178
surveillance footage 178
survive 110
suspect 90
suspense 116
sustainable 150
swamp 154
swear an oath 100
swear s.o. in 100
swipe 174
syllable 121
synchronize/synchronise 174

T

tablet 174
tabloid 128
take hostage 90
take place 112
take power 94
take responsibility 10
take up 32
target 14; 150
target group 130
target sports 32
tariff 44
tax 100
technique 160
technological advance 174
televise 32
tell off 10
temperate 155
temperature 168
territory 183
terrorist attack 100
test 76
testify 90
theft 90
third-person narrator 116
thought-provoking 134
threat 90
threaten 106
thrill 32
tissue 160
tough measure 32

tour operator 54
tournament 33
tower block 140
toxic 150
track 178
trade 46
trade agreement 46
trade barrier 46
trade union 64
trafficking 90
tragedy 118
transaction 174
transit country 50
transition 10; 183
transmit 136
transplant 160
transport 44
transportation 54
travel agency 54
travel industry 14
treatment 170
trial 90
troops 111
truce 111
trustworthiness 27
tuition fee 67
turn up/down 174
turning point 116
TV listings 136
TV set 136

U

undercut 37
undergo a change 112
undergraduate/graduate 67
underground 140
undocumented 50
unemployment 44
university 66
unrestricted access 126
uphold 107
urban growth 140
urbanization 140
urine sample 33

V

vaccine 160
values 27
verse form 121
veto a bill 107
via 174
vice-president 107

victim 90
victory 101
viewer 136
violate 26
violence 33
virus 170
vocational education/
    qualification 67
vocational training 64
voluntary work 10
vomit 170
vote 101
voter 101
voting/polling booth 102
vulnerable 174

W–Y

wage 64
wage war 109
warfare 111
waste 150
water sports 33
water supply 150
wavelength 14
weapon 91
weed 161
white-collar worker 64
widowed 6
wilderness 155
wildfire 150
wireless 174
withdraw 102
word processing 174
work experience 64
workforce 64
working hours 64
World Cup 33
World Trade Organization
    (WTO) 46
worship 26
wound 111
yield 161